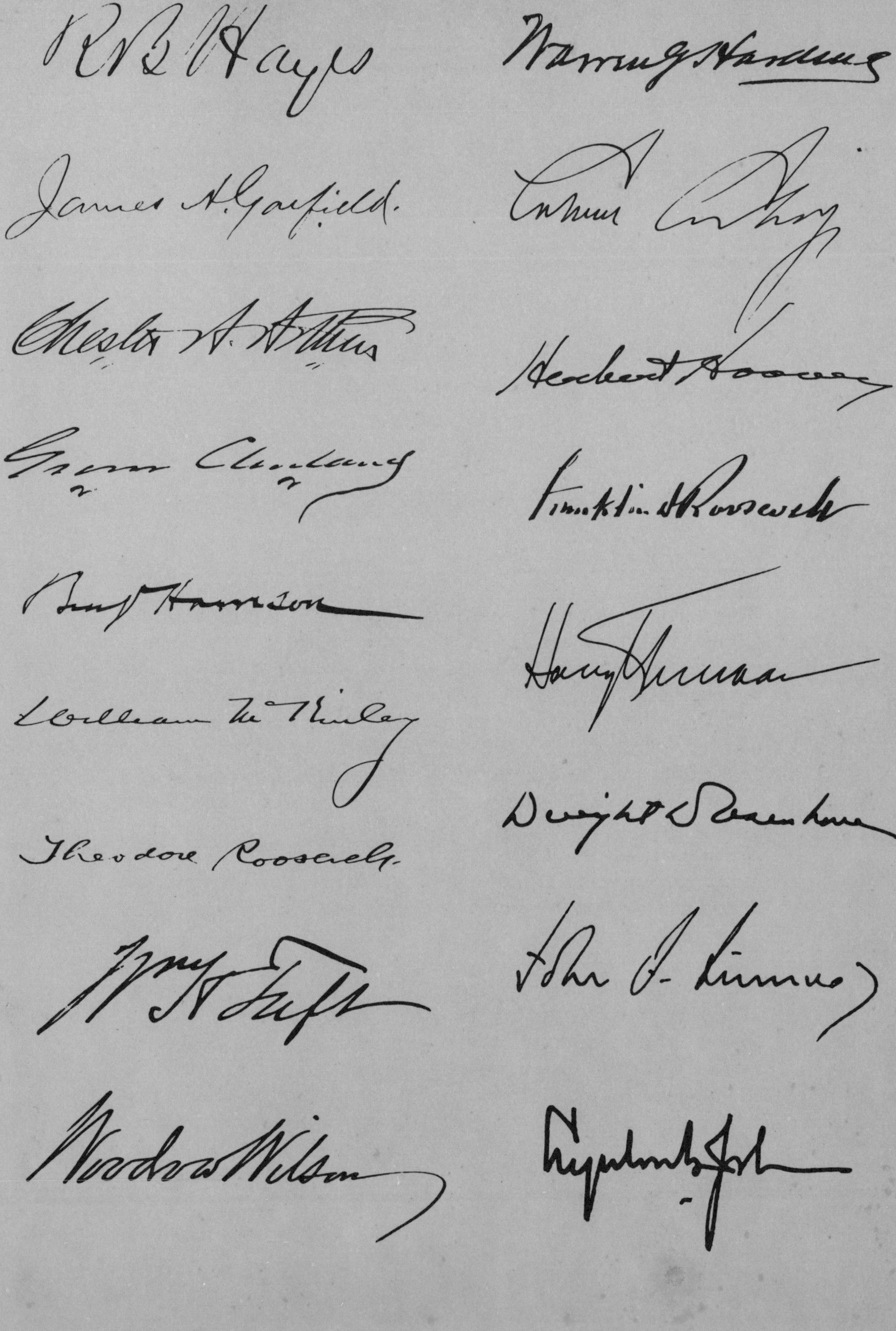
R B Hayes
James A. Garfield
Benj Harrison
Theodore Roosevelt
Woodrow Wilson
Warren G Harding
Herbert Hoover

Wyatt Blassingame has never laid eyes on a President of the United States and has divided his votes evenly between Democratic and Republican candidates since he reached voting age. The son of schoolteacher parents, he was born in Demopolis, Alabama, and spent his early years in small Alabama towns where his parents' collection of books often became the town library. Since graduating from the University of Alabama, he has worked as a reporter, served as a Navy Lieutenant during World War II and made a career of writing. He has some 600 short stories and magazine articles, four adult novels, and over twenty children's books—mostly on American history—to his credit. He and his wife now live on an island off the Gulf Coast of Florida.

Ted Lewin, was born in Buffalo, New York, where President McKinley was assassinated. He was educated at Pratt Institute and he supported himself there by wrestling professionally. He won the Dean's medal on graduation. Since then he has worked as an illustrator for most of the major magazines and for several text book publishers. *The Look-It-Up Book of Presidents* constitutes two first for him. It is his first children's book and makes him the first artist to have portrayed all the Presidents. Mr. Lewin now lives in Brooklyn with his wife, Betsy.

The Look-It-Up Book of PRESIDENTS

by Wyatt Blassingame
Illustrated by Ted Lewin

Random House · New York

Dec 25, 69

Daddy:

Thanks for
the education
I know you worked
hard to send me to school
but I think it is helping me
be a good wife to Jim and
thats all I want to be

Love Pat & Jim

For Phillip Scott

who, like any American, may be President someday.

Or even ambassador.

Published in the United States by Random House, Inc., New York,
and simultaneously in Canada by Random House of Canada Limited, Toronto.

Library of Congress Catalog Card Number: 68-23656

Manufactured in the United States of America

Printed by Copifyer Lithograph Corp., Cleveland, Ohio

Designed by Janet Townsend

The President of the United States

Who can be President? Any natural-born citizen of the United States who is over the age of thirty-five and has lived in the United States for fourteen years or more.

What does a President do? The President is the chief executive of the United States. According to the Constitution, he "shall take care that the laws be faithfully executed." From time to time, he informs Congress in his State of the Union message what has been done and what needs to be done.

Although he cannot force Congress to act, he can suggest a program for them to consider. And, as leader of his political party, he can often see that program is carried out, when his party has a majority of seats. He can also prevent Congress from acting by using the Presidential veto.

The President plays the chief part in shaping foreign policy. With the Senate's approval, he makes treaties with other nations and appoints ambassadors. But he can also make executive agreements with other nations without approval of the Senate.

He nominates members of the Cabinet, Supreme Court justices, and many other high officials. These nominations must be approved by the Senate. However, he can fill thousands of other important posts under his own power.

The President is Commander-in-Chief of the Armed Forces and commissions officers in all branches of the service.

How is the President elected? The voters of each state choose a number of electors equal to the number of Senators and Representatives they have in Congress. The Electoral College, made up of the electors from every state, then chooses the President by majority vote. The electors usually vote for the candidate supported by the voters of their state. When there are more than two Presidential candidates and none gets a clear majority, Congress selects the President from the three candidates who had the most votes.

How long is the President in office? The President is elected to a term of four years. Since Article XXII of the Constitution became effective in 1951, no President may be elected to more than two terms.

When does the President take office? The new President takes office at noon on January 20 of the year following his election, on taking this oath of office:

"*I do solemnly swear (or affirm) that I will faithfully execute the office of President of the United States, and will, to the best of my ability, preserve, protect, and defend the Constitution of the United States.*"

George Washington

1st President of the United States 1789-1797

Born: February 22, 1732, near Fredericksburg, Virginia.
Died: December 14, 1797, at Mt. Vernon, Virginia.

April 30, 1789. General George Washington stood on the balcony of Federal Hall in New York City. Around him were many of the greatest men in America. In the street below a huge crowd stood quietly.

Slowly, solemnly, George Washington took the oath that made him the first President of the United States. He leaned forward and kissed the Bible on which he had sworn. Then from the men on the balcony and from the street below a great roar went up. "Long live George Washington, President of the United States!" Everyone was sure they had chosen their best leader to be the first President.

But what was the job of the President? Was he to be a dictator who ran the country to suit himself? Was he to be a figurehead who signed laws that Congress passed? The answers lay in the hands of the tall man on the balcony. He would shape the job, and with it the future of the new nation.

Washington realized this. He once said, "I walk on untrodden ground. There is scarcely any part of my conduct that may not hereafter be drawn into precedent."

George Washington's father was a well-to-do farmer. The boy spent much of his time outdoors. He grew tall and lean with a fair skin that sunburned easily. He became an excellent horseman. He went to school only off and on, and only until he was about 15. But he was always good at figures. At 14 he surveyed his father's farms just for fun.

At 15 George went with a party of surveyors to work in the Shenandoah Valley. Later he worked for a time as public surveyor of Fairfax County, Virginia. Then, when he was 21 years old, his military life began.

At this time the American Colonies still belonged to England. Canada belonged to France. French soldiers from Canada had built forts in the Ohio Valley on land claimed by England. The Governor of Virginia appointed young George Washington to ride through the wilderness and tell the French they would have to leave.

One French fort was near what is now Waterford, Pa. Here the French commander greeted Washington politely but said the Ohio

Valley belonged to France and the French soldiers would not leave.

A year later the British General Edward Braddock led a small army against the French and Indians. Washington was Braddock's aide-de-camp. The British General knew nothing about fighting in the wilderness. His troops marched straight into an ambush and were badly defeated. But in the fighting Washington showed the qualities of a first rate officer. He had a cool, exact, thoughtful courage. He was not hurt, but two horses were killed under him and his uniform was cut by four bullets. It was largely due to his leadership that part of the British army escaped.

After this battle Washington was made commander of all the Virginia troops. For several years he led them in small frontier fights against the French and Indians. Then, when he was 26 years old, he quit the army. He had met a rich young widow named Martha Dandridge Custis. He married her and settled down.

For the next 15 years Washington spent most of his time at his farm called Mount Vernon. He was a good farmer. He raised horses and cattle, apples, peaches and pears. This was one of the happiest times in his life. He had no children of his own, but he loved the little girl and boy who were Martha's children by her first husband.

At this time great changes were taking place in the American Colonies. The Colonies still belonged to England, but many Americans thought they were not being fairly treated. They thought the Colonies should have more to say about their own government. At last, the quarrel grew into a war.

On April 19, 1775, British soldiers clashed with Americans at Lexington and Concord. The Revolutionary War began. Because of his military experience, George Washington was appointed Commander in Chief of the American Army. The fact that he was a Southerner was very important. Most of the army outside Boston was Yankee and Congress wanted a general who would attract Southerners to join. Congress also wanted a wealthy man as general, since they could not afford to pay him.

Today most military men believe George Washington was a good general but not a great one. His army lost more battles than it won. But it was never destroyed. It was never captured. Washington himself said that as long as the Americans could keep an army in the field, the British could not win. And somehow Washington kept his army in the field. This was where he was truly great. He had a strange ability to inspire men. His soldiers did not have enough guns or enough am-

munition. They were often ragged and hungry. Washington lived and suffered with them. And in some way he made them feel that as long as he led them they could not lose. By the sheer strength of his character he held his army together. He kept it fighting.

At this time France also was at war with England. With the help of a French fleet, American soldiers trapped a British army under Lord Cornwallis at Yorktown, Virginia. On October 21, 1781, Cornwallis surrendered. The peace treaty was not signed for almost two years, but Yorktown was the end of the actual fighting. The Colonies had won. Now they were free and independent states.

During the war American soldiers had been poorly paid. After the war they expected some reward from Congress, but Congress was slow to act. The soldiers became angry. Some of them wanted Washington to lead a revolt and make himself king. He could easily have done so. But Washington refused to turn against his own government. He refused to be king. Once more he quit the army and went back to his home at Mount Vernon.

Washington was happiest at home with his family. But soon the new nation was in trouble. Each of the states considered itself independent.

There was danger they might start fighting among themselves.

In the summer of 1787 men from the different states met in Philadelphia to try to draw up plans for a new government. The meeting was called the Constitutional Convention. At it were many of the most important men in America. George Washington was elected Chairman of the Convention. His job was to hold the Convention together as he had held his army together. All summer he kept these men working.

The plan they finally drew up was the Constitution of the United States. With some changes it is the same basic plan by which we are governed today. It called for a strong central government headed by a President. George Washington was elected the first President. He received every vote.

Washington did not believe in government by political parties. He thought his job was to be President of all the people, and he appointed to his Cabinet the best men he could find. These men, however, did not always agree with Washington, and they did not always agree with one another. Alexander Hamilton, Secretary of the Treasury, wanted a very strong central government run only by men who were both rich and intelligent. Thomas Jefferson, Secretary of State, believed most powers should belong to the states. Also, he had more faith in the people than did Hamilton.

Political parties began to form around these two men. Persons who agreed with Hamilton were called Federalists. Those who agreed with Jefferson were called Republicans. (Much later this party would change

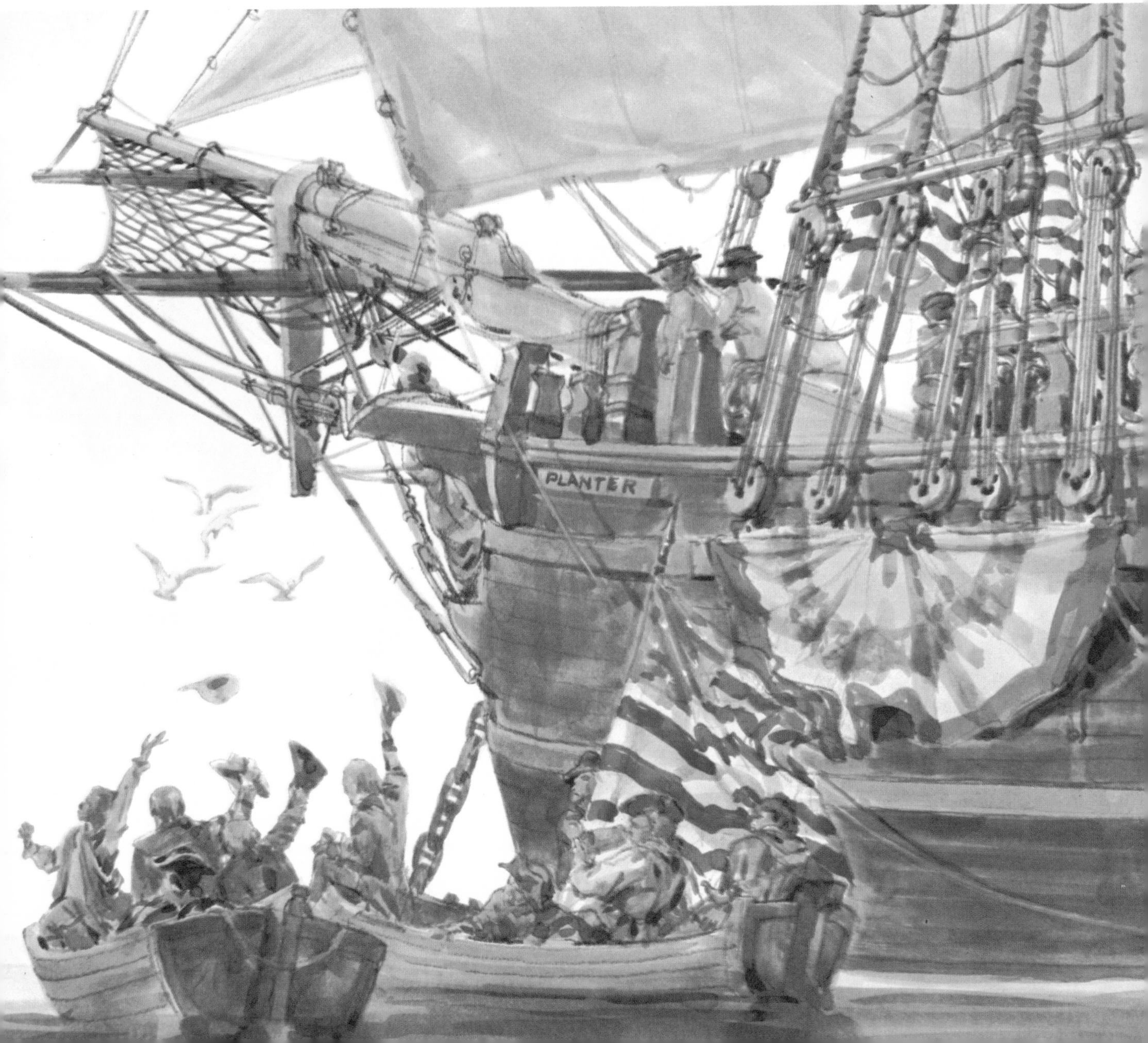

its name to Democrat, and a new Republican Party would be formed.)

With his great personal influence, Washington might have made himself dictator. He might have told Congress what laws to pass and what not to pass. On the other hand, he might have left everything to Congress, if he had wished. Instead, he set a middle course. Some later Presidents have made the office of President stronger, some weaker. But all have been influenced by the course that Washington set.

Washington was not a brilliant President. Thomas Jefferson said Washington's mind "was slow in operation . . . but sure in conclusion." He never acted "until every circumstance, every consideration was maturely weighed . . . but when once decided upon, going through with his purpose whatever obstacles opposed."

Washington believed that as the chief officer of a new nation he should make a dignified appearance. For this reason he dressed very formally. Whenever he traveled he went in a handsome carriage pulled by beautiful horses. In his own behavior he was naturally dignified. He could laugh at jokes, but he rarely told any. He inspired awe rather than friendship, even in the great men around him.

In 1793 Washington was elected to a second term. Now the nation was facing new and ever more difficult problems.

France and England were once more at war. Many Americans now wanted to help France. Washington wanted to keep his country at peace. The United States, he said, should stay out of European troubles.

More trouble came when the Federal Government placed a tax on whiskey. Many persons did not believe the Federal Government had the right to put such a tax on individuals. They refused to pay. In what was called the Whiskey Rebellion, government tax collectors in Washington County, Pennsylvania, were badly beaten. The Governor of Pennsylvania refused to punish the rebels.

Washington knew that no government could last unless it had the power to enforce its laws on individuals. He sent troops into Pennsylvania and put down the rebellion. He proved that the Federal government could enforce its laws.

Now for the first time a number of people began to complain about Washington. Even so, most people wanted him to be President for a third term. But he was 65 years old. He was physically tired. He refused a third term and went back to the life he loved at Mount Vernon.

He did not enjoy it for long. On December 12, 1799, he was caught in a snowstorm while riding around his farm and became sick. Two days later he died.

The news of his death came as a great shock to the whole world. Even the British whom he had fought had learned to admire and respect him. Thomas Jefferson, who often disagreed with Washington, said, "He was indeed, in every sense of the words, a wise, a good, and a great man." But it was one of Washington's old soldiers who put the nation's feelings into words. Washington, said General Lighthorse Harry Lee, was "first in war, first in peace, and first in the hearts of his countrymen."

And so he has been ever since.

John Adams

2nd President of the United States 1797-1801

Born: October 30, 1735, at Quincy, Massachusetts.
Died: July 4, 1826, at Quincy, Massachusetts.

John Adams was born on a small farm near what is now Quincy, Mass. His parents were not well educated, but they sent John to Harvard University. Afterward he taught school briefly, then studied law. He was still studying law when he heard a speech that influenced the rest of his life.

The speech was by a man named James Otis in 1761.The American Colonies still belonged to England. James Otis was speaking against a law passed by the British Parliament. Otis said this law was unfair because the Colonies had no one in Parliament to speak against it. If a law was unfair and unjust, the people had a right to oppose it. They had a right to make their own laws.

Young John Adams was deeply moved. Liberty, the freedom to make ones own laws—these were the things for which Adams' ancestors had come to America. They were things in which he believed with his whole heart.

John Adams became one of the leaders in the American independence movement. From 1774 to 1778 he was a member of the Continental Congress. He was there on June 7, 1776, when Richard Henry Lee of Virginia moved "that the united Colonies are, and of right ought to be, free and independent States."

Adams was a member of the committee appointed to write the Declaration of Independence. Thomas Jefferson did most of the actual writing; but it was John Adams who led the debate in Congress to have the Declaration passed.

In 1778 John Adams wrote a Constitution for his home state of Massachusetts. Later it would serve as one of the models for the Constitution of the United States.

During the Revolutionary War Adams worked for his country in Europe. He was one of the men who drew up the final peace treaty with England. After that he served as the United States ambassador to England.

In 1789 when George Washington was elected the first President,

John Adams was elected Vice President. He was not happy in his new job. He liked to talk, but, as Vice President, he had to be quiet while others talked. Once he wrote his wife that the job of Vice President was "the most insignificant office that ever the invention of man contrived."

In 1789 when George Washington refused a third term, John Adams was elected President. Like Washington he did not believe in political parties. He thought of the President as a "patriot king" and not as the leader of one party. But political parties had already been formed. Adams soon found himself in trouble.

John Adams stood somewhere in the middle, but he had been elected by the Federalists. The Federalist Party, led by Alexander Hamilton, believed in government by a small group of rich and powerful men. The Republican Party (which later changed its name to Democrat) believed in government by the mass of people.

Adams was a good lawyer and a very smart man. But he was not a good politician. He was proud and stubborn. Also, he was a poor judge of men. All the men he appointed to his Cabinet were Federalists. They were more loyal to Alexander Hamilton, the leader of the party, than to Adams. Hamilton was not a member of the government, but for a while he seemed to be more powerful than the President.

At this time France was at war with England and other European countries. Hamilton wanted the United States to have close ties with England even if it meant war with France. Adams, like Washington, did not want the United States closely tied with any European country. Also, he wanted peace if possible. He sent men to talk with the French Government.

The French refused to talk with the Americans unless the United States paid them money. Adams wanted peace, but not at any price. He would not pay a bribe to France. Instead, he asked Congress to order new warships. A Navy Department was established for the first time. John Adams is sometimes called the Father of the United States Navy. There was no declaration of war, but American and French warships fought whenever they met.

The Federalists wanted war with France. Against the wishes of Hamilton and his Cabinet, Adams sent more men to France to talk

peace. This time the French Government was willing to meet with them and a war that might have destroyed the young nation was avoided.

Near the end of Adams' term as President the Government moved from Philadelphia to the new capital city of Washington, D.C. The unfinished White House was cold and damp. But on his second night in the White House John Adams wrote: "I pray Heaven to bestow the best Blessings on this House and all that shall hereafter inhabit it. May none but honest and wise men ever rule beneath this roof."

In saving his country from war, Adams had angered the leaders of the Federalist Party. In the election of 1801 they turned against him and he was defeated. Except for his pride, Adams had not wanted to be reelected. He went back to his home in Massachusetts. He died there on the 4th of July, 1826, exactly 50 years after the Declaration of Independence.

He was a true patriot; a brave and stubborn man. Before his death he had said the words on his tomb ought to read: "Here lies John Adams who took upon himself the responsibility of the peace with France in the year 1800."

Thomas Jefferson

3rd President of the United States 1801-1809

Born: April 13, 1743, in Albemarle County, Virginia.
Died: July 4, 1826, at his home at Monticello, Virginia.

When Thomas Jefferson was born in 1743, Albemarle County, Virginia was still frontier country. Here Peter Jefferson, Thomas' father, was a moderately well-to-do farmer and surveyor. Thomas' mother came from one of the best families in Virginia.

Thomas Jefferson was tall and thin with a freckled face and sandy hair. He had one of the most brilliant minds in American history. Before he was 30 years old he had studied half a dozen languages, law, mathematics, science, philosophy. He was a self-taught architect who designed some of the most beautiful homes in the world. He was an inventor. He invented the first swivel chair, the dumb waiter, the American system of money. He was a fine musician.

When he was 26 Jefferson was elected to the Virginia Legislature. Strangely, he was not a good public speaker, so instead of making speeches he wrote many letters and articles. Often these were about the growing trouble between the Colonies and Great Britain. One of his articles was about what Jefferson called "The Rights of America." It made Jefferson's name known in all the Colonies.

In 1772, he married Martha Skelton. Three years later, he was elected to the Continental Congress. Because of his fame as a writer, he was appointed to write the Declaration of Independence.

During the Revolutionary War Jefferson was first a member of the Virginia Legislature, then Governor of the State. He worked hard to pass a law guaranteeing freedom of religion. It was the first law of its kind in America.

After the war, Jefferson served as Minister to France. Then when the new Constitution was adopted and Washington elected President, Jefferson was appointed Secretary of State.

From the first Jefferson was afraid that the United States might some day become a dictatorship. He believed with all his heart that the people should, and could, govern themselves. Raised on the frontier, Jefferson hoped America would become a nation of farmers needing few laws.

Alexander Hamilton, Washington's Secretary of the Treasury, loved his country as much as did Jefferson. But he did not agree with Jefferson's ideas of what made a good government. He believed the English system, headed by a king or at least a lifetime President, would be best. Both men were completely honest in their views. But Jefferson believed Hamilton's ideas would turn the United States into a dictatorship. Hamilton believed Jefferson's ideas would end in mob rule.

Jefferson did not, at first, intend to form a political party. But soon he became the leader of the men who agreed with him. They began to be called Republicans. (Years later this party would change its name to Democrat.) The men who agreed with Hamilton became known as Federalists. Nobody planned it, but this was the beginning of the party system in the United States.

President Washington agreed more often with Hamilton than with Jefferson. At the end of Washington's first term, Jefferson resigned and went back to Virginia.

When Washington refused to serve a third term, John Adams was elected President, Thomas Jefferson Vice President. Adams belonged to the Federalist Party, Jefferson to the Republican Party. This mixup happened because the men who wrote the Constitution had not thought about political parties. They planned for the man who got the most votes to be President and for the man who got the next most votes to be Vice President. Later the Constitution would be changed so that the President and Vice President would always belong to the same party.

Adams served only one term, then Jefferson was elected President. Because he believed the country should be run as cheaply as possible, he cut down on the army and navy. Because he wanted to represent the mass of the people, he did not wear handsome uniforms as Washington had done. Nor did he ride in a big carriage pulled by many horses. Instead he walked, or rode horseback.

At this time France owned most of the vast, unknown land west of the Mississippi River. At New Orleans France controlled the land on both sides the river. This meant France could close the river to American boats if she wished. But this river traffic was very important to American settlers west of the Appalachian Mountains. So in 1803 Jefferson tried to buy New Orleans from France. To his surprise,

Napoleon, the French Emperor, offered to sell the whole Louisiana Territory from the Mississippi River to the Rocky Mountains.

Jefferson believed that a President had no powers except those put down in the Constitution. And nothing in the Constitution said a President could double the size of the United States. But Jefferson also believed that the future of the U.S. lay in the west. Here was too good a chance for his country to miss. Jefferson signed the treaty buying the Louisiana Territory. Then he asked Congress for permission to do what he had already done.

About this time there was trouble with the Barbary pirates who lived along the northern coast of Africa. For a number of years their warships had been capturing American merchant ships in the Mediterranean Sea and holding the crews for ransom. It was cheaper to pay than to fight, but Jefferson would not take this way out. He sent the tiny U.S. Navy to attack the pirates. After losing several sea battles, the pirates were forced to allow American ships to pass through the Mediterranean in peace.

In 1804 Jefferson was elected for a second term.

France and England were once more at war. English warships often captured American merchant ships to keep them from trading with France. To avoid war, Jefferson got Congress to pass a law forbidding American ships to trade with either England or France. English trade, however, was big business in the New England states. Merchants began to lose money. After a while Jefferson realized the law was doing his country more harm than good. One of his last acts as President was to ask Congress to repeal it.

Despite his unpopular law, Jefferson might have been reelected if he wished. But he was always afraid that some day the office of President might be turned into that of a dictator. So he did not believe that any man should be President more than two terms. Also, he had never been really happy as President. So he refused to be elected for a third term. He went back to the beautiful home called Monticello that he had designed.

His service to his country, however, was not yet over. He planned and helped build the University of Virginia. He brought together the teachers and helped decide what subjects should be taught. He gave advice to the men who followed him as President of the United States.

Thomas Jefferson died on the same day as John Adams, July 4, 1826. It was exactly 50 years after the Declaration of Independence which he had written. Jefferson wrote the words to go on his own grave:

"Here was buried Thomas Jefferson, author of the Declaration of Independence, of the statute of Virginia for religious freedom, and father of the University of Virginia."

He did not even mention having been President of the United States.

James Madison

4th President of the United States 1809-1817

Born: March 16, 1751, at Port Conway, Virginia.
Died: June 28, 1836, at Montpelier, Virginia.

Most of James Madison's youth was spent in Orange County, Virginia. He was a thin, sickly child. He took all his lessons at home until he was 18. He never weighed much more than a hundred pounds and he stood only five-and-a-half feet tall. Washington Irving once called him "a withered little apple-John."

At last, his health improved and he went to Princeton University, where he often worked over his books for 16 and 17 hours a day. Even so he had some time to take part in the long talks between students and teachers. Many of these dealt with the growing troubles of the American Colonies with Great Britain. Madison was always on the side of the Colonies.

It took Madison only two years to graduate from Princeton. For a while then he thought about being a preacher. He was sincerely religious. At the same time he believed deeply in religious freedom. Religion and government, he thought, ought to be kept completely separate.

Instead of going into the church, young Madison went into politics. During the Revolution he served in the Continental Congress. After the war was over he was one of the first men to recognize the great problems facing the new country.

At this time the nation had no real central government. Each state considered itself more or less independent. Madison knew that if the country was to get along, it must have a central government with more power. He and other leaders urged that a convention be called to form such a government.

This convention met in Philadelphia in the summer of 1787. James Madison was one of the members. Later another member of the Convention wrote about Madison: "Every person seems to acknowledge his greatness. . . . In the management of every question he . . . took the lead."

The plan finally settled on became the Constitution of the United States. With some changes it is the same plan by which we are governed today.

When the new government was formed, James Madison was elected to the House of Representatives. Here he led the fight to add the first 10 Amendments to the Constitution. These are known today as The Bill of Rights and James Madison is often called the Father of The Constitution.

James Madison did not get married until he was 43 years old. His bride, Dolly Todd, was 17 years younger than Madison and weighed a good bit more. They made an odd-looking couple; the young, laughing, pretty girl and the thin, sick-looking man. And yet they made a very happy couple.

In 1801 Thomas Jefferson appointed Madison Secretary of State. For eight years the two men worked closely together. When Jefferson retired, Madison was elected President.

France and England were still at war with one another. Whenever possible, England captured American ships to keep them from trading with France. France captured American ships to keep them from trading with England.

Some of the young men in the Republican Party wanted a war with England. Madison could not control them. Although he had a brilliant mind, he was not a great leader of men.

These War Hawks, as they were called, were using the British attacks on American ships only as an excuse. What they really wanted was to capture Canada from England and Florida from Spain, which was an ally of England. In June, 1812, they talked Madison into asking Congress to declare war on England. This was called the War of 1812.

The war was not popular with the ship owners, most of whom lived in New England. It was supposed to protect their shipping. Actually it kept them from trading and making money. Also, many of the owners belonged to the Federalist Party. They called it "Mr. Madison's War."

At first things went badly for the United States. American armies were defeated along the Canadian border. American ships won a few brilliant victories, but they could not stand up to the big British fleet. The city of Washington was captured by the English, who burned the White House and the Capitol building. Then the British fleet sailed up Chesapeake Bay to attack Baltimore. Here, however, they were turned back. And here an American lawyer named Francis Scott Key who watched the battle wrote *The Star Spangled Banner*.

Madison had begun peace talks with the English almost as soon as he began the war. Finally in 1815 a peace treaty was signed in Europe.

The news took so long to reach the United States that the final battle was actually fought after peace had been declared. This was the Battle of New Orleans and the Americans, under General Andrew Jackson, won a smashing victory.

The peace treaty settled none of the problems that had caused the war. But because of the victory at New Orleans most Americans felt they had won the war.

At the end of his second term James Madison was glad to retire and go back to his home in Virginia. He had done his best as President. But his truly great service to his country had been as "Father of the Constitution."

James Monroe

5th President of the United States 1817-1825

Born: April 28, 1758, in Westmoreland County, Virginia.
Died: July 4, 1831, in New York City.

James Monroe was the last of the Revolutionary leaders to become President.

Like all the Presidents before him except John Adams, he was born in Virginia. He was tall and rawboned with a quiet, natural dignity. When he was 16, Monroe left home to go to William and Mary College. Two years later, in 1776, he left college to join the Revolutionary Army.

After the war, Monroe studied law under Thomas Jefferson. Although Jefferson was 15 years older, the two men became close friends. When Monroe was only 24 he was elected to the Virginia Legislature. Later he served in the U.S. Senate and then as Governor of Virginia.

In 1811 President James Madison appointed Monroe Secretary of State. In fact, for a while during the War of 1812, he was both Secretary of State and Secretary of War at the same time. In 1816 he was elected President.

The War of 1812 was over. The Federalist Party, which had opposed Monroe, had not helped to fight the war and was no longer popular. To find how the people did feel and what they wanted, James Monroe went on a trip across the country. Although styles had changed, he still wore old-fashioned knee britches and shoes with buckles on them. People remembered that he had been an officer in the Revolution and wounded in battle. Everywhere he went he was met by cheering crowds. In Boston a newspaper wrote this was the "era of good feeling." Soon the Presidency of Monroe came to be known as the Era of Good Feeling.

Even though the war was over, both the United States and Great Britain still had warships on the Great Lakes. There was always a chance that fighting might start again. President Monroe suggested that each country limit its warships on the lakes to a few very small ones. England agreed. This agreement has helped keep the peace ever since.

At this time Florida still belonged to Spain. But there were only a few Spanish settlers in Florida. American settlers in Georgia looked at the open land to the south and wanted it.

Seminole Indians from Florida sometimes raided the Georgia farms. The Spanish Government was not strong enough to stop them. So President Monroe sent General Andrew Jackson with a small army to fight the Seminoles. Jackson did not find many Seminoles. But he did capture Pensacola from the Spanish, even though the United States was not at war with Spain.

President Monroe ordered Jackson to withdraw his troops, but it was clear the U.S. could capture Florida at any time. So the two governments signed a treaty by which Spain gave Florida to the U.S. In return the United States gave up its claim to have bought Texas as part of the Louisiana Purchase. As part of the agreement, the United States agreed to pay $5,000,000 that some Americans claimed was owed to them by Spain.

In 1820 James Monroe was elected to a second term. He got every vote in the Electoral College except one. The one man who voted against Monroe said he did not think anybody but Washington should ever get every vote.

Until about the time of Monroe's first election, Spain had owned

most of South and Central America. But as Spain grew weak, one South American country after another declared its independence. Spain herself could not stop them. But in 1823 Spain asked the help of France and other European countries. Together they might reconquer the newly free countries of South America.

President Monroe did not like the idea. He declared that the United States was not going to meddle in the affairs of any European country. But the United States did not want any European country meddling in American affairs. No new colonies were to be started in the Americas. Any nation that tried to start one would be considered unfriendly.

This became known as the Monroe Doctrine. It has been a basic doctrine of the United States ever since.

When his second term was over, Monroe went back to his home in Virginia. He died while visiting his daughter in New York in 1831. The day was the 4th of July. Of the six Presidents who took part in the Revolution, three of them—Thomas Jefferson, John Adams and James Monroe—died on a 4th of July.

John Quincy Adams

6th President of the United States 1825-1829

Born: July 11, 1767, at Quincy, Massachusetts.
Died: February 23, 1848, in the Speaker's room at the House of Representatives, Washington, D.C.

John Quincy Adams was seven years old when the Battle of Bunker Hill was fought. It was a day he would never forget. Already he loved his country with fierce pride. During all his long life he would serve the United States loyally and honestly. But that service would be marked by tragedy as well as triumph.

John Quincy was the son of John Adams, second President of the United States. He was the only son of a President to become President himself.

When John Quincy was 11 years old, his father was sent to France as an American diplomat. He took John Quincy with him. During the next few years the boy went to school in France and Germany. At 14 he went to Russia to serve as secretary for the American Minister. The following year he worked as secretary for his father. At this time John Adams was helping write the peace treaty that ended the American Revolution.

When the fighting ended, John Quincy Adams went to Harvard University. He graduated in 1787, then studied law. But soon he was sent by President Washington to represent the United States in one European country after another.

When Thomas Jefferson became President, John Quincy Adams returned to the United States. A year later he was elected to the Senate as a member of the Federalist Party. But John Quincy Adams, like his father and George Washington, never believed in political parties. He voted for what he thought was right, whether the party liked it or not. Soon he began to agree with the Republican Party more often than with the Federalists. As a result he lost his office after one term.

President Madison, a Republican, sent John Quincy to Europe in 1814. There he helped write the peace treaty that ended the War of 1812. When James Monroe became President in 1817 he appointed John Quincy Adams Secretary of State.

John Quincy Adams became one of the truly great Secretaries of

State. He was a short, heavy-set man with heavy-lidded eyes, a cold mouth. He did not make friends, but he made the best possible bargains for his country. He helped settle a quarrel between the United States and England over the Oregon Territory. He wrote the treaty by which the United States won Florida. He played a very important part in framing the Monroe Doctrine.

In the Presidential election of 1824 there were four important candidates. In the electoral college, Andrew Jackson got the most votes, Adams was second, but no one got a majority. This meant the final choice had to be made in the House of Representatives. Adams was chosen. It was an honest election, but Jackson and his followers were angry. They accused Adams of making crooked deals to win the election.

Adams' four years as President were probably the most unhappy years of his life. As Secretary of State he could fight for what was best for his country. But as President he could not fight to defend himself. He said it was beneath the dignity of a President to answer the lies

told about him. He loved his country deeply, but he was so cold and harsh that people did not understand it. Many people admired his intelligence, but almost no one admired the man himself. His sharp tongue made enemies. He was lonely. In the early mornings he went for long, lonely walks or swam in the Potomac River.

Adams wanted the United States to become a center of learning. He asked Congress to build a national university. He asked for roads and canals and a Naval Academy. Later most of these things would be done. But Adams could never get along with Congress. As a result they refused to do what he asked. In the election of 1828 he was defeated and Andrew Jackson was elected.

Deeply hurt by his defeat, Adams went back to his home in Massachusetts. But then the people of his area elected him to Congress. Some people said he would be disgraced by serving in Congress after he had been President. Adams' answer was typical of him. He said that no man was disgraced by serving his country.

For the next 17 years John Quincy Adams served in Congress. He fought for the things he had always believed in. He helped establish the Smithsonian Institution. He fought against slavery and for civil rights and free speech. He was one of the nation's finest Congressmen. He was at his desk on February 21, 1848, when he fell unconscious. Two days later he died.

Andrew Jackson

7th President of the United States 1829-1837

Born: March 15, 1767, in the Waxhaw settlement, South Carolina.
Died: June 8, 1845, at his home near Nashville, Tennessee.

Andrew Jackson was the first President born in a log cabin of a poor family. His father and mother had come from Ireland only two years before his birth. His father died before he was born; his mother died when he was 14. He had little formal education, but he learned to read. When he was nine years old he read the Declaration of Independence aloud for a group of frontiersmen who could not read. When some of these frontiersmen formed a Revolutionary Army unit, the boy watched their crude drilling. At 13 he could no longer just watch. He joined the army himself. Already an excellent horseman, he carried messages from one unit to another. A year later, he was captured by the British. One day, Jackson was cut across the head when he refused to clean an English officer's boots. The blow left a scar on his face and on his feelings. For the rest of his life he hated the English and was fiercely proud of America.

After the war Jackson studied law, then moved farther west to the frontier village of Nashville, in what is now Tennessee.

The frontier suited Jackson. Tall, straight and handsome, he was quickly popular. He gambled on horses, cockfights and business. He made money and lost it and made it again. Reckless and hot-tempered, he was wounded twice in duels. Once he killed a man he thought had insulted his wife.

When the people in Tennessee raised an army to fight the Creek Indians, Jackson was elected General. He had no military training, but he proved to be an excellent general. He defeated the Indians. The next year, 1814, he was made a general in the Federal Army. In the last battle of the War of 1812 he defeated the British at New Orleans and became a national hero.

At this time Florida still belonged to Spain. Seminole Indians living in Florida sometimes made raids across the Georgia border. President Monroe sent Jackson with a small army to stop these raids.

The hot-headed Jackson said the Spanish were protecting the Seminoles and that Florida really ought to belong to the United States.

So he not only chased the Seminoles into Florida, he attacked and captured the Spanish city of Pensacola. This could have led to war with Spain—and that would have been all right with Jackson. However, Secretary of State John Quincy Adams managed to keep peace.

In 1824 the people of Tennessee nominated Jackson for President. It may be that Jackson did not really want to be elected. He had already been elected to Congress three different times, and each time had quit before his term was up. He was quoted as saying, "Do you think that I am such a darned fool as to think myself fit for the presidency? No sir . . . I can command a body of men in a rough way, but I am not fit to be President."

In the election Jackson was defeated by John Quincy Adams. Jackson's friends told him he had been cheated. This was not true, but Jackson believed his friends. From that day he set out to defeat Adams as he might have set out to win a battle.

By the next election in 1828 the old Federalist Party was all but dead. The Republican Party, founded by Thomas Jefferson, was also breaking into groups. Of these, the more democratic group was led by Jackson. It was called the Democratic Republican Party, but dropped the word "Republican" and became the Democratic Party. The more conservative group was led by John Quincy Adams. It was called the National Republican Party, then later changed its name to Whig. And so the United States had two new political parties.

At this time people from all over the United States were moving west. New states were coming into the Union and new frontiers being opened. There was a feeling that now was the time to find new, more democratic rules of government. The old rule that only men who owned property could vote was being changed.

Jackson himself was a frontiersman. He came from a poor family. To the people moving west, looking for new land and a new life, he was a hero. In the election of 1828 Jackson was swept into office.

From all over the country the common people who admired Jackson came to hear him take the oath of office. Then they went crowding into the White House to have a party. Many of the old, well-to-do families in the east thought that the rule of "King Mob" had started.

Most of the Presidents before Jackson had left law-making up to Congress. Jackson said it was his job to help people get the laws they wanted, and no others. Time and again he vetoed laws passed by Congress. He urged the passage of others. People who did not like Jackson said he was trying to act like a king. They called him King Andrew

the First. But most of the people, especially in the west, liked what he did. In 1832 he was elected to a second term.

In South Carolina many people did not like a law that had been passed by Congress. The State Legislature passed its own law which said that the Federal law would not be enforced in South Carolina.

Andrew Jackson believed in States Rights, but only so far. He said no one state had the right to decide which national laws it would obey and which it would not. If this were so, the Union itself would fall apart. Jackson said he would enforce the national laws even if it meant war with South Carolina. He got ready to fight. Fortunately a compromise was worked out. But Jackson had showed, as Lincoln would later, what a strong President could do to save the Union.

From the modern point of view Jackson had many faults. He believed in slavery. He thought that the only good Indian was a dead Indian—or at least one pushed out of the white man's territory. But no President except Washington did as much to make the office of President strong. He was one of the few Presidents to finish his second term as popular as when he began his first one.

Martin Van Buren

8th President of the United States 1837-1841

Born: December 5, 1782, at Kinderhook, New York.
Died: July 24, 1862, at Kinderhook, New York.

Martin Van Buren's father was a farmer and tavern keeper at Kinderhook, New York. Martin was born there. He was the first President to be born after the United States became an independent nation.

Van Buren went to school for only a few years. When he was 14 he got a job in a lawyer's office, and at 21 became a lawyer himself.

He was a successful lawyer. He was also interested in politics, and held a number of state offices. He used these offices to give jobs to people who would vote for him and for his political friends. In this way he built up a large following. In 1821 he was elected to the U.S. Senate and was reelected in 1827.

At this time Andrew Jackson was running for President. Van Buren was a very smart politician, but he did not inspire the fierce love and loyalty that Andrew Jackson did. Van Buren knew this. And he knew his own political future might depend on Jackson. So he worked hard to help Jackson win the election. When Jackson was elected he appointed Van Buren Secretary of State.

Van Buren made a good Secretary of State. Even so, there were other men in Jackson's Cabinet who were much more famous. No one suspected that Van Buren would ever become President.

Jackson and Van Buren became very close friends. When Jackson ran for a second term he asked that Van Buren be made Vice President. And it was largely because of Jackson's help that Van Buren was elected President in 1836.

At this point one of the worst depressions in history hit the country. One business after another failed. Banks had to close their doors. All over the country hungry men and women walked the streets without jobs.

There were many causes for this depression. Some of the things done by Andrew Jackson had helped. Chiefly, however, the depression was caused by a wild spirit of gambling that had swept the country. Everywhere men had been buying land with borrowed money, hoping the price of the land would go up. Men had borrowed money to start

new businesses, then needed more money to keep them going. So it was the people themselves who were largely to blame. Nobody, however, likes to blame himself. So the people turned on Van Buren.

Van Buren was trying hard to be a good President. Yet he was easy to blame. He was a small man with a red face and white, mutton-chop whiskers and he was a dapper dresser. Because he liked to eat well, his enemies said he drank foreign wines, used gold forks and silver plates.

This was the same kind of gossip that Van Buren had once spread to help Andrew Jackson defeat John Quincy Adams. Now it was enough to make hungry people without jobs vote against Van Buren. In the election of 1840 he was defeated by William Harrison.

William Harrison

9th President of the United States March to April 1841

Born: February 9, 1773, at Berkeley, Virginia.
Died: April 4, 1841, at Washington, D.C.

When William Henry Harrison was 14 he went to Hampden-Sidney College. He studied the Greek and Latin classics and liked to read them all his life. Later he studied medicine, because his father wanted him to. But when his father died, Harrison quit school and joined the army. For several years he served on the northwest frontier and fought against the Indians.

Harrison was only 27 when he was appointed Governor of the Indiana Territory. He served in this office for 12 years. During this time the famous Indian chief Tecumseh led his followers on the warpath. Governor Harrison with about 1,000 soldiers clashed with the Indians on the banks of the Tippecanoe River. It wasn't really a very big or important battle, but it made Harrison famous. He was given the nickname "Old Tippecanoe."

During the War of 1812 Harrison served as a General in the American Army. He won one of the few United States victories on the Canadian border. He served briefly in Congress. Then for several years he lived on his farm in North Bend, Ohio. He thought he had left public life forever.

However people still remembered "Old Tippecanoe."

In 1840 Van Buren ran for a second term. The Whigs named only one man to run against him. It was Harrison.

Harrison had never taken a very large part in politics. He was much better known as a military hero than a politician. But the Whigs needed a popular hero, not a politician. They did not even say what Harrison or the Whig Party believed in. They just ran against Van Buren's record as President.

At this time the country was in the middle of a very bad depression. Many people were out of jobs. The Whigs blamed this on Van Buren. They said he was rich and did not care about the people. At the same time they said nothing about Harrison's well-bred background. Instead, they talked about him as an Indian fighter. Part of Harrison's home in North Bend, Ohio, had once been a log cabin. So the Whigs said their hero lived in a log cabin. They said Van Buren lived in a "palace," as they called the White House and drank French wine while Harrison drank plain hard cider. This became known as the "Log cabin and hard cider campaign."

None of this had anything to do with which man would make the best President. But it was a time when Americans wanted frontiersmen and Indian fighters for their heroes. In 1840 William Henry Harrison was elected President.

Harrison was hardly in office before long lines of people were asking him for jobs. He was a kindly man. He wanted to help and he worked hard. But he had been President less than a month when he caught a bad cold. A few days later he died. He was the first American President to die in office.

John Tyler

10th President of the United States 1841-1845

Born: March 29, 1790, at Greenway, Virginia.
Died: January 18, 1862, in Richmond, Virginia.

John Tyler's father was a Governor of Virginia and a friend of Thomas Jefferson. The boy grew up believing with all his heart in States Rights. He thought that the powers of the Federal Government should be very limited.

He graduated from William and Mary College when he was 17. At 21 he was elected to the Virginia Legislature. Later he served in the House of Representatives, as Governor of Virginia, and in the U.S. Senate. But outside his own state he was little known.

The Whig Party nominated Tyler for Vice President mainly because he was from the South. Harrison was from the West, and the Whigs wanted a Vice President who could help get the Southern vote. Tyler was a good-looking, courteous, soft-spoken man from a good family. He was well liked in his home state, and the Virginia vote was important. So the Whigs nominated him. They didn't expect him ever to be President. Nobody bothered to think about what kind of President he might make.

His record in Congress showed clearly what he believed in. Like his father's friend, Thomas Jefferson, he believed the Federal Government should keep out of the States' business. He had always voted against spending Federal money for such things as roads and harbors. He had originally been a Democrat, not a Whig, and had supported Andrew Jackson for President. But Tyler thought Jackson took too much power for the Federal Government. Tyler turned against him. It was largely because of this that he was regarded as a Whig, although none of his ideas had changed. Always his ideas were his own rather than those of either party.

Even so, the Whigs were not really worried, at first. Until this time no President had ever died in office. Many persons thought that on Harrison's death Tyler did not really become President, but only "Acting President" until the next election. They thought this would be a sort of caretaker's job. Also, Tyler kept in his Cabinet the same men Harrison had appointed. These were all good Whigs. They were sure Tyler would do as they told him.

It didn't take long to find out they were wrong.

Daniel Webster, the Secretary of State, told Tyler that President Harrison had agreed to let a majority of his Cabinet make the important decisions. Tyler told Webster that he, as President, would make his own decisions. The Whigs wanted to start a national bank. Tyler didn't believe in national banks and vetoed the law. The Whigs rewrote it. Tyler vetoed it again.

The Whig leaders met and declared that Tyler was no longer a member of the Whig Party. Every member of the Cabinet except one quit. Tyler appointed a new Cabinet.

And that is the way things went during most of the four years Tyler was President. The Whigs hated him. The Democrats didn't want him. Many politicians put party loyalty ahead of everything else. To such men Tyler was a traitor. He was known as the President without a party.

Tyler was in his 50's and looked younger. His wife died soon after he became President and he married again. His second wife, Julia Gardiner, was 30 years younger than he was, but that didn't bother Tyler. He was the first President to be married while in office.

Tyler did one important thing as President. At that time Texas had broken away from Mexico and wanted to join the United States. But it was legal to own slaves in Texas. Many people in the North did not want another slave state in the Union but Tyler was from Virginia and he believed in slavery. He asked the Senate to approve a treaty taking Texas into the Union. The Senate refused.

In the election of 1844, Tyler was anxious to be reelected for two reasons: he was ambitious, and he wanted to make sure Texas came into the Union. But neither the Whigs nor the Democrats wanted him. When he tried to form a third party, it failed.

The Democrats, however, did say they were in favor of Texas joining the Union. They won the election. And then Congress, without waiting for the new President to take office, passed the bill admitting Texas. Tyler signed it, one of his last acts as President.

When Tyler's term was over, he went back to Virginia. Later, as the Civil War was beginning, he was elected to the Confederate Congress. He died, however before that Congress ever met.

James Polk

11th President of the United States 1845-1849

Born: November 2, 1795, in Mecklenburg County, North Carolina.
Died: June 15, 1849, at his home in Nashville, Tennessee.

James Polk was born in North Carolina but when he was 11 years old his family moved to Tennessee. This was still frontier country. James Polk's father was a farmer, but the boy was too sickly to do much work on the farm. He rarely took part in the rough games of other boys. Instead he spent most of his time reading. At the University of North Carolina he graduated with top honors, then studied law.

From the first Polk was interested in politics. He was elected to the U.S. House of Representatives and from 1835 to 1839 he was Speaker of the House. Polk was a great admirer of Andrew Jackson and worked to pass the laws Jackson wanted.

Polk quit Congress to run for Governor of Tennessee. He was elected, but in 1841 he was defeated for a second term. In 1843 he was defeated again. At this point it might have seemed that his career was over. He had never been really well. He was in pain much of the time. Certainly most men would have given up. But James Polk had a lonely, cold, fierce, driving spirit that would not let him quit.

In 1844, when the Democratic Convention met to name a candidate for President, most people thought Martin Van Buren would be chosen. A few people thought James Polk might be named for Vice President, but most people did not know much about him.

To win the nomination a candidate needed two-thirds of the votes. At first Van Buren had more than half the votes, but he could not get two-thirds. It began to look as if nobody could be named. Then Andrew Jackson came out for Polk. Since nobody else could win, the convention agreed on Polk as a compromise. This made him the first "dark horse" candidate for President—that is, a man not well known before he ran for the office. The Whig candidate was Henry Clay, one of the most famous men in America at that time.

Texas became the big issue in the campaign. Polk and the Democratic Party wanted Texas in the Union. Henry Clay also wanted Texas, but he was sure it would cause war with Mexico. And he did not want war. So Clay never made clear just where he and the Whig Party stood.

Another question in this election was who owned the Oregon Territory. Oregon was the name given to all the land between California and Alaska west of the Rocky Mountains. Both Great Britain and the U.S. claimed it. Now Polk and the Democrats said it must be made part of the U.S. even if it meant war.

In the 1840's many Americans were moving west. Long wagon trains streamed over the Oregon and Sante Fe Trails. A newspaper man had written that it was the "manifest destiny" of the United States to be one country from coast to coast. The phrase caught on. Everybody talked about the manifest destiny of the young nation. The country was growing and needed more room. So the people elected the "dark horse" James Polk. As soon as the election was over, Congress voted to annex Texas. They didn't even wait until Polk took office.

Even so James Polk said there were still four things he wanted to do as President. They were: to lower the tariff—a tax paid on foreign goods brought into the United States; to set up a national treasury; to settle the question of the Oregon Territory; and, above all, to make California a part of the Union.

Congress quickly passed laws lowering the tariff paid on foreign goods, and starting the Treasury. But for a while it looked as if there might actually be a war with England over the Oregon Territory. Polk did not want to fight England. England did not want to fight either, so it was fairly easy to reach an agreement. It was agreed to run the Canadian border straight west to the Pacific, splitting the Oregon Territory between the United States and Canada. This is the border we have today.

That left California, the most important of all to Polk. Yet actually he knew very little about California. He had read that it was a lush and beautiful land. He knew it belonged to Mexico, but Mexico had only a few settlers there. What really bothered Polk was the fear that England or France might take over this land if he did not grab it first.

Polk tried to buy California. Mexico would not sell. He tried again, but it only made the Mexicans angry.

Then James Polk used methods of which no American can be proud. First, he tried to stir up a revolution among the few American settlers in California. But they were too few and too far away. So Polk deliberately forced Mexico into a war. He did not say the war was over California. Instead, he sent an army into Texas. Mexico still claimed that Texas belonged to it. However, Mexico did not fight so long as the American army stayed north of the Nueces River. Up to this time most persons considered the Nueces as the southern border of Texas. Polk now claimed Texas went to the Rio Grande and he sent the army there. The Mexican Government was forced to fight. And this gave Polk an excuse to send warships and an army to capture California.

Polk knew the Mexican Government was weak and could not hope to win a war. Even so, the war turned out to be longer and more bloody than he expected, but finally Mexico was forced to surrender. In the peace treaty the United States agreed to buy from Mexico what is now all of California and Nevada, and part of Utah, Arizona and New Mexico.

President Polk refused to run for a second term. As President he had worked hard. After four years in office he was both tired and very sick. He went back to his home in Nashville, Tennessee, and died a few months later.

There can be no doubt that what James Polk accomplished was good for his country. It can be wished he had found a more honorable way.

Zachary Taylor

12th President of the United States 1849-1850

Born: September 24, 1784, in Orange County, Virginia.
Died: July 9, 1850, at Washington, D.C.

Zachary Taylor was raised in the little frontier village of Louisville, Kentucky. His father had been an officer in the Revolutionary War. All his childhood Zachary heard stories about drilling and fighting.

When he was 22 years old Taylor joined the army as a private. Two years later he was made lieutenant. He fought in Indian campaigns, and in the War of 1812. Later he fought against the Indian chief Black Hawk and against the Seminoles in Florida. During the Seminole War Taylor was made General.

Texas became part of the Union in 1845. At this time most people thought the Nueces River was the southern border of Texas. But President James Polk sent General Taylor with an army across the Nueces to the Rio Grande. This brought on the Mexican War.

General Taylor was not a great general, but he was a pretty good one. In the Battle of Buena Vista, he defeated a Mexican Army four times as large as his. With his other victories this made him a national hero.

It was a hero the Whig Party wanted for a Presidential candidate in 1848. They had two to choose from: General Taylor and General Winfield Scott. Both were professional soldiers. Except for that, they had almost nothing in common. Scott dressed in handsome uniforms. His boots were always polished. His soldiers had nicknamed him "Old Fuss and Feathers." Taylor wore the same dirty clothes he wore on his farm. His soldiers called him "Old Rough and Ready."

In the young, tough frontier nation of 1848 Old Fuss and Feathers did not have a chance against Old Rough and Ready. The Whigs nominated Taylor as their candidate and he was elected.

No man ever became President knowing less about what he was supposed to do. Taylor was simply a soldier, used to giving and taking orders. He was totally honest, blunt, straightforward. And he did not know how to work with politicians.

At this time, thousands of Americans were pouring west. They wanted the new western territory to be made into states. But would slavery be allowed in the new states, or not?

The South wanted more slave states. Most of the country did not. Some Southern Congressmen began to talk about leaving the Union.

Most people had expected President Taylor to favor slavery. He had been born in the South. He owned slaves on his plantation in Louisiana. But above everything else he wanted to protect the Union. He called in the Southern Congressmen who were talking about secession. He told them that if they tried to break up the Union he, personally, would lead an army against them.

Slowly Congress worked out a compromise on the question of slavery in the new states. President Taylor did not like it. He might have vetoed it. But, suddenly, on the 4th of July, 1850, he became ill. Five days later he died.

Millard Fillmore

13th President of the United States 1850-1853

Born: January 7, 1800, near the present Summerhill, New York.
Died: March 8, 1874, at Buffalo, New York.

Millard Fillmore's father had a small farm in the Finger Lakes section of New York State. It was not much more than a clearing hacked out of the woods on the frontier. Here the boy worked until he was 15.

Young Fillmore went to a one room school whenever he could. This was not often. At 18 he was a tall, good-looking boy, out of place among the seven and eight year olds in the same room. The teacher was a pretty red-haired girl named Abigail Powers. She taught him so well that when he was 20 he moved to Buffalo, New York, and got a job teaching. At the same time he studied law. Before long he was admitted to the bar and married Abigail.

Fillmore was quickly successful. In 1832, he was elected to Congress as a member of the Whig Party. In Congress he voted against admitting Texas to the Union because it permitted slavery. In 1848, the Whig Party chose him to be Vice Presidential candidate. He was elected.

As Vice President, Fillmore presided over one of the most important debates in American history. Would the new western territories be free states or slave states? Both of the parties, the Democrats and the Whigs, were split on the question. The Senators from the South wanted

slavery. Most of the Senators from the North wanted the territories to be free. Some Southerners began to talk about seceding from the Union.

Senator Henry Clay, from Kentucky, offered a compromise. Later it became known as the Compromise of 1850. Its main point was that California would come into the Union as a free state. In return there would be a law called the Fugitive Slave Act. By this law an owner could follow his runaway slave into a free state and recapture him, and it would be against the law to help a slave run away.

President Fillmore did not like slavery. But he thought the Compromise law was fair to both sides. He hoped it would settle the question of slavery and hold the Union together. Largely because of President Fillmore's influence, Congress passed the Compromise of 1850.

This compromise made many people in the North more opposed to slavery than ever.

Because Fillmore signed the Compromise of 1850 many Whigs in the North turned against him. As a result he was not nominated by the Whig Party for reelection. And before long the whole party began to fall apart. Millard Fillmore was the last Whig President.

President Fillmore did do one thing of lasting importance. For 200 years Japan had refused to trade or to have anything to do with other countries. In 1853 President Fillmore sent Commodore Matthew Perry with United States ships to pay a visit. Commodore Perry got the Japanese Emperor to agree to let some American ships visit the country for trade. This became known as the "opening" of Japan.

Mrs. Fillmore as wife of the President also did some things for the first time. She bought the first cookstove and set up the first library in the White House.

Franklin Pierce

14th President of the United States 1853-1857

Born: November 23, 1804, at Hillsboro, New Hampshire.
Died: October 8, 1869, at Concord, New Hampshire.

Franklin Pierce came from a well-known New England family. His father was twice Governor of New Hampshire. During his second term, Franklin was elected to the State Legislature, then he was elected

to the United States House of Representatives, and later to the United States Senate. He was the youngest member of the Senate.

As a young Congressman Pierce had married the pretty daughter of the President of Bowdoin College. Two of their three sons died while still very young. Mrs. Pierce was often sick. She was shy and did not like the social life in Washington. Finally she persuaded her husband to quit the Senate and go back to New Hampshire.

When the Mexican War started Pierce enlisted as a private. President Polk promptly made him a colonel, then a general, although he had no military experience.

In 1852 a convention met in Baltimore to name the Democratic Party's candidate for President. At this time Pierce was little known outside his home state. Everybody thought the candidate would be one of the leaders of the party. But none of these well-known men could get enough votes to win. Finally, on the 49th ballot, Franklin Pierce was named as a compromise. But he won the election and became President.

As President, Pierce wanted to get more land for the United States. He wanted to take over Hawaii, which was still independent, but nothing came of it. He tried to buy Cuba from Spain, but only made Spain angry. But he did manage to buy a narrow strip of land from Mexico. Today this forms the southwestern corner of New Mexico and all of southern Arizona. It was called the Gadsden Purchase.

At this time a senator named Stephen Douglas wanted to build a railroad from Chicago to the Pacific. He wanted it to go through Kansas because he owned land there. Other senators wanted it built in other places. In order to get Southern votes, Senator Douglas proposed a law called the Kansas-Nebraska Act. This law would do away with the Missouri Compromise of 1820. That compromise had drawn a line north of which slavery would never be legal. The new Kansas-Nebraska Act would allow each territory to decide for itself whether or not to have slavery, no matter how far north it was.

Many men knew that this Kansas-Nebraska Act would cause bitter trouble between the North and South. Somehow President Pierce did not seem to understand this. Instead he pushed the law through Congress.

Now each territory could vote on slavery for itself. Men from the South rushed into Kansas so they could vote for slavery. Men from the North rushed in to vote against it. The fighting was so bitter that the new territory was often called "Bleeding Kansas."

But all over the nation people were arguing about the right and wrong of slavery. By the end of Franklin Pierce's first term the nation was hurtling toward its most terrible tragedy, the Civil War. A new anti-slavery party, called the Republicans, was formed. And Northerners in Pierce's own Democratic Party would not nominate him for a second term. He went back home to New Hampshire. But even there he was not popular any more.

James Buchanan

15th President of the United States 1857-1861

Born: April 23, 1791, near Mercersburg, Pennsylvania.
Died: June 1, 1868, near Mercersburg, Pennsylvania.

James Buchanan's father owned a small country store near the border of Pennsylvania and Maryland. The boy learned to add and subtract and keep books by clerking in the store. Later, he studied law and went into politics. He was over six feet tall, broad shouldered, dignified. When he was 23 years old he was elected to the State Legislature. At 30 he was elected to Congress. He belonged to the Federalist Party, but this party was slowly breaking up. Buchanan became a Democrat.

President Polk appointed Buchanan his Secretary of State. He helped settle the problems of the Oregon Territory and the Mexican War. Buchanan believed the United States ought to get more and more territory. Once he wrote that the U.S. should try to buy Cuba from Spain. If Spain would not sell, Buchanan said, the U.S. should take Cuba by force.

By the election of 1856 slavery had become the biggest problem facing the United States. Many persons in the North wanted to end slavery altogether, North and South. Southern slave owners wanted slavery made legal in all the territories.

The new Republican Party was against slavery. Their candidate was John C. Fremont. Their slogan was "Freedom, Freemen, and Fremont."

The Democratic Party did not want to take any strong stand on slavery one way or the other. They hoped this would anger nobody, North or South, and win votes. Buchanan had been out of the country during much of the argument over slavery. Nobody was quite sure

just where he stood. So the Democrats made Buchanan their candidate. It was a close election, but Buchanan won.

Buchanan had been in office for only two days when the U.S. Supreme Court handed down a decision that highly pleased the slave owners in the South. It was called the Dred Scott decision. The Supreme Court said that slavery had to be legal in all United States territory not yet made into states.

Buchanan agreed with this decision. He did not like slavery, but he thought that under the Constitution, the Union had no right to stop it. He hoped that the Dred Scott decision would end the argument. Instead, it only made matters worse. When new problems arose, Buchanan sided with the South in the hope that this would keep the Southern states from seceding.

By the election of 1860 slavery was the one all-important question. The Democratic Party split over the question. One group favored the North, one the South. But neither group nominated Buchanan. The Republican Party nominated a tall, gaunt man named Abraham Lincoln.

Lincoln won, but there was a period of several months before he took office. For James Buchanan these months proved the hardest of his four years as President.

One Southern state after another seceded from the Union. With all his heart Buchanan wanted to hold the Union together. But he was not sure what to do. He did not believe that any state had the right to secede. At the same time he did not believe the Union had the right to force a state to stay in the Union. Also, he was hopeful—he was always hopeful—that if he did nothing, the states that had left the Union would decide to rejoin.

And so he did nothing.

On March 4, 1861, Abraham Lincoln became President. A few weeks later the Civil War began. And at long last James Buchanan made up his mind. The North, he said, must back President Lincoln "to a man," no matter what the price.

Abraham Lincoln

16th President of the United States 1861-1865

Born: February 12, 1809, in Hardin County, Kentucky.
Died: April 15, 1865, in Washington, D.C.

Abraham Lincoln's father was a ne'er-do-well farmer who drifted from one place to another along the frontier. When Abe was eight years old the family moved to Spencer County, Indiana. Abe helped to build the cabin they lived in. It had only three walls. On the open side a fire had to be kept going day and night.

Lincoln had little schooling. "There were some schools, so called," he said. But all they taught was "readin', writin' and cipherin'. . . . Of course when I came of age I did not know much. Still somehow, I could read. . . ." And he loved to read. There were few books on the frontier, but Lincoln borrowed all he could. At night he read by the light of an open fire.

In time Lincoln's family moved from Indiana to Illinois. By now Abe was six feet four inches tall, thin, awkward, homely looking. His coarse black hair stood up on his head. Outdoor work had made his arms and shoulders unusually strong.

Lincoln's voice was high pitched. It sounded strange coming from such a tall, powerful body. Yet even as a boy he had a great gift for telling stories. He could make people laugh. And people liked him. It was not that he inspired hero worship as Andrew Jackson had done. He was too awkward and homely for people to think of him as a hero. But people trusted him. They believed in him.

As a young man Lincoln got a job on a flatboat going to New Orleans. Back in Illinois he got a job in a country store. The store failed and he got other odd jobs. He split rails. He worked as a surveyor. Finally a friend told him he ought to be a lawyer. It was easier to be a lawyer then than it is now. Lincoln borrowed books and studied. He was always quick to learn. He became a lawyer and was elected to the State Legislature. Then he was elected to Congress.

In Congress Lincoln proposed one important law. He said the government should buy all the slaves in the District of Columbia and set them free. The law did not pass, but it showed how Lincoln felt. He believed slavery was wrong. But he did not believe slavery could be

abolished without payment to the slave owners.

Lincoln did not win a second term in Congress. He went back to Illinois to practice law. For a few years he took little part in politics.

It seemed as if Lincoln's public life was over. But the question of slavery was being debated more and more throughout the country. New territory was being opened in the west, new states coming into the Union. Should these be free or slave?

Lincoln was opposed to the spread of slavery. More than that, he wanted to help the poor of any race. He knew what it was to be poor. He began to make speeches in favor of keeping the territories free. "New free states," he said, "are places for poor people to go and better their condition." They should not be turned over to rich slave owners.

In 1858 the Republican Party asked Lincoln to run for the Senate against Stephen Douglas. Douglas was in favor of letting each new state decide for itself whether or not to have slaves. In a famous series of speeches, Lincoln and Douglas debated this question. Douglas won the election. But these Lincoln-Douglas Debates made Lincoln famous.

Because of this the Republican Party named him to run for President two years later.

It was a bitter election. The Democratic Party split in two, one part in the South, one in the North. A new third party tried to find some kind of compromise. Lincoln and the Republicans came out against the spread of slavery.

The election was held in the fall of 1860. Lincoln won, but he was not to take office until March 4, 1861. In the meanwhile one Southern state after another voted to leave the Union and set up a new government. President Buchanan let them go, not knowing what else to do.

On March 4, 1861, Abraham Lincoln became President. A month went by and he took no action. There were a number of reasons for this. Several of the border states had not yet decided whether to secede or stay in the Union. Lincoln wanted to hold these states if he could. Also there were a number of persons in the North who did not believe either the Union or slavery were worth fighting about. Lincoln knew that if he started a war himself, many of these people would not support it. But his determination to save the Union never wavered.

On April 12, 1861, Southern soldiers fired on the Union-held Fort Sumter in Charleston, South Carolina. A great wave of patriotism swept the North. Lincoln knew that now the people would support him.

The next four years were probably the most desperate in United States' history. In these years Abraham Lincoln proved himself to be a great President. Even so, there was a while when he made many mistakes. He tried one general after another before he found a really good one. He did not get along too well with his own Cabinet. Some of them did not understand this tall, gaunt man who always looked as if he had bought his clothes second-hand from a man four inches shorter than he was.

Lincoln's great gift was his ability to make the common people understand and believe in what he was doing. His purpose was to save the Union because to him the Union was not just a group of states that had got together to form a government. It was the only important democratic government in the world. If it were destroyed, it would mean that free men were not able to govern themselves. The fight to save the Union was the fight to save free government all over the world.

Somehow he made the people understand this. He made them understand the wrongness of slavery. He made them understand that the war touched on the great principle that all men are created free and equal before God.

In the past Lincoln had not believed that, under the Constitution, the Federal Government had the right simply to declare an end to slavery. Yet what good would it do to hold the Union together by force if slavery, which had caused the war in the first place, was not ended? Lincoln thought more and more about this as the war went on. Finally, "The moment came," he said, "when I felt that slavery must die that the nation might live." And so on September 22, 1862, he issued his Emancipation Proclamation. This stated that on January 1, 1863, all slaves in any state still in rebellion against the Union would be free.

The Emancipation Proclamation did not actually free any slaves at all. It applied only to the rebellious states where Lincoln had no power to enforce it. Slavery was still legal in several of the border states that had not left the Union. Lincoln believed that to end slavery in these states, the Constitution would have to be amended. He began to work toward such an amendment. (When it did pass, it was the 13th Amendment.)

Although the Emancipation Proclamation itself did not end slavery, it did make clear one important reason for the war. And it gained sympathy for the North throughout the civilized world. In this way it helped toward final victory.

For Lincoln the entire war was a period of much personal grief. Always he was aware of the death and suffering on both sides. Men saw him walking the streets at night, alone, deep in thought. Sometimes in rain or fog he wore a shawl around his shoulders, his long neck bent forward, the lines of his bony, ugly face drawn deep with sorrow.

By the fall of 1864 it was clear the North was winning the war. Lincoln was easily elected to a second term.

Lincoln never wanted revenge upon the South. Instead he said, "Blood cannot restore blood, and government should not act for revenge." He only wanted to restore the Union, as quickly and peacefully as possible. In the second inaugural address he told how he believed the nation should act:

"With malice toward none, with charity for all, with firmness in the right, as God gives us to see the right, let us strive on to finish the work we are in, to bind up the nation's wounds, to care for him who shall have borne the battle, and for his widow and his orphan—to do all which may achieve and cherish a just and lasting peace among ourselves and with all nations."

This was his dream. It was not to be.

On April 9, 1865, General Robert E. Lee surrendered to Lincoln's General U. S. Grant at Appomattox Courthouse. On the night of April 14, five days later, President and Mrs. Lincoln went to see a play at a Washington theater. During the play an actor named John Wilkes Booth stepped into the box behind Lincoln and shot him in the back of the head. Next day one of the greatest men in all American history lay dead.

It is probable that Booth, in some crazed way, believed he was helping the South. The actual result of Lincoln's death was the exact opposite. Had Lincoln lived, he might have brought the South back into the Union with the least possible bloodshed and bitterness. Without Lincoln, some of the worst men, both North and South, came into power. The evil they did lives long after them.

Andrew Johnson

17th President of the United States 1865-1869

Born: December 29, 1808, at Raleigh, North Carolina.
Died: July 31, 1875, at Carter Station, Tennessee.

Andrew Johnson's father worked as a sort of handyman in a tavern in Raleigh, N.C. His mother was a maid in the same tavern. Johnson's father died when the boy was three years old and his mother had to take in washing to help feed her children. Young Andy never went to school. As a young boy he was apprenticed to a tailor. Probably it was here, somehow, that he learned to read. But he hated his master. When he was 16 he ran away to the little town of Greenville, Tennessee, and went into business for himself.

He was a good tailor and he began to make money. When he was 18 he married Eliza McCardle. She was only 16, but she had been to school. She taught her husband to write, and helped him with his reading.

Johnson was a stocky young man with a hard mouth and no humor in his eyes. He rarely laughed, but he had a great drive to get ahead in the world. He began to walk several miles back and forth to a school that let him take part in student debates. He had a big, booming voice, a mind like a steel trap, and a tongue like a whip. Many of the students, far better educated than Johnson, were afraid to debate with him.

Although he had little humor, Andrew Johnson was capable of love and had a deep sense of duty. As soon as he had made a little money he brought his mother, his brothers and sisters to live with him. Always he thought of himself as the champion of the poor and the weak against the rich and the strong. He went into politics.

Most of the people who lived in Johnson's part of Tennessee were farmers or small businessmen. They elected Andrew to the town council before he was 21. Then they elected him mayor. He was only 33 when elected to Congress. At 45 he was Governor of Tennessee. He served two terms, and was elected to the U. S. Senate.

Andrew Johnson's father had never owned slaves. In fact, he had never owned anything. But Johnson believed that slavery was guaranteed by the Constitution. Also, he was a Democrat. In the Senate he voted with the South on almost every issue.

After Lincoln was elected, the Southern states left the Union, Tennessee with them. As the states seceded, every Southerner left Congress—except one. Andrew Johnson. "I voted against Lincoln," Johnson said, "I spoke against him. I spent my money to defeat him. But still I love my country."

Johnson became something of a hero in the North. And in the election of 1864 the Republicans wanted to be a "Union" party, not one representing only part of the country. So when Lincoln ran for a second term, the Republicans nominated Andrew Johnson for Vice President. They never expected him to be President. But Lincoln was murdered, and Johnson *was* President.

Johnson, like Lincoln, did not want to take revenge on the Southern states. He wanted them brought back into the Union as quickly and easily as possible. Although some of the former leaders of the Confederacy were not pardoned, he gave a pardon to all Southerners who would promise loyalty to the Union.

This had been Lincoln's plan. But in the U.S. Congress there were a number of men, called Radical Republicans, who were opposed to it. They believed the South had to be punished for having left the Union. They refused to admit the newly elected Southerners to Congress.

Certainly the South was partly to blame for the trouble that followed. Although slavery had been abolished, laws were passed which said no Negro could vote or sit on a jury. In some states no Negro could have a business of his own. He could be arrested and forced to work for white men. In some places he was not even allowed to walk into a town without permission from a white man.

Cruel laws of this sort did not help Johnson in his efforts to help the South. Instead they made more and more people in the North agree with the Radical Republicans. More Radical Republicans were elected to Congress.

Congress began to discuss the 14th and 15th Amendments to the Constitution. These made citizens of the former slaves and guaranteed them the right to vote. Next Congress divided the South into five military districts. The Federal Army was sent in to take command. Southern officials were thrown out of office and new elections were held under military control.

In these elections the Negroes were allowed to vote, but many white Southerners were not. Also the old leaders of the South were not allowed to run for office. As a result, some poor whites and former slaves who could neither read nor write were elected. They knew

nothing about running a government and the state governments fell apart.

There were a number of reasons why the Radical Republicans passed these extreme laws. Some Congressmen honestly wanted to help the Negroes. Some of them simply wanted to punish the South. But many of them voted for purely political reasons. Most white Southerners had been Democrats. The Radical Republicans did not want them to get back in power. Some Radical Republicans even wanted the Constitution changed to make sure the Republican Party would always be in power.

In the South the white people now had almost no lawful way to protect themselves. As a result, some began to use unlawful ways. Groups such as the Ku Klux Klan tried to force Negroes back into the old way of life by frightening them. If fear was not enough, the Klansmen sometimes killed. They attacked Northern whites who had come into the South. Some of these, called Carpetbaggers, were there only to try to make money from an unhappy situation. But the Klan also attacked and sometimes murdered good men who had come South to teach the former slaves.

Andrew Johnson did not have Lincoln's great power to persuade and lead the people. He made speeches asking for moderate treatment of the South. But his own speeches were not moderate. Indeed, they were so violent that he lost voters rather than gained them.

Finally Congress decided to get rid of President Johnson—the only time in the history of the United States that this has happened. There were no lawful grounds for the charges brought against Johnson. They were based on anger rather than reason. But it was a time when anger, not reason, ruled much of the nation.

During the trial one of the lawyers defending Johnson told Congress: "He is a man of few ideas, but they are right and true, and he can suffer death sooner than yield up or violate one of them." It was a good picture of the President. Even so, the U.S. Senate voted 35 to convict Johnson, 19 to acquit him. However, the law required a two-thirds majority to convict. So Andrew Johnson missed being put out of office by one vote.

Johnson's term ended soon after this. He went back to Tennessee. And six years later he was once more elected to the U.S. Senate. In the meanwhile some of the Senators who had once voted against him had come to admire his courage. They stood and clapped for him when he entered the Senate.

It may have been a proud moment for the old fighter. But maybe not. He himself had not changed. He made a speech in which he defended what he had done as President, and lashed out at those who had opposed him.

It was his last big speech. A short time afterward he became sick and died.

Ulysses Grant

18th President of the United States 1869-1877

Born: April 27, 1822, at Point Pleasant, Ohio.
Died: July 23, 1885, at Mount McGregor, New York.

When he was 39 years old Ulysses S. Grant was clerking in a small town store for $50 a month. Before this he had quit or been fired from every job he ever had. He drank too much. Most people thought of him as a bum.

Three years later, in 1864, Grant was a Lieutenant General in command of all the U.S. Armies. In 1868 he was elected President of the

United States. He served two terms, and seven years after he left office he was flat broke once more.

It is the strangest, up-and-down career of any American President.

His name wasn't even U.S. Grant to begin with. When he was 17 years old, his father, who owned a tannery and farm near Point Pleasant, Ohio, managed to send him to West Point.

The Congressman who appointed him to the Military Academy thought his name was Ulysses Simpson. (Simpson was his mother's maiden name.) So U.S. Grant was the name under which he was registered at West Point. And the name stuck.

As a young lieutenant, Grant served under General Zachary Taylor in the Mexican War. He admired General Taylor's coolness in battle and the sloppy way he dressed. Later, as a commanding general, Grant would be just as cool and almost as sloppy as the man he admired.

Grant was married shortly after the Mexican War. But when he was ordered to duty in the west he could not take his family with him. He began to drink. Finally his commanding officer told him he must either quit drinking or resign. Grant resigned.

Back home, his wife's father gave him a small farm near St. Louis. Grant liked to farm. But the land was poor and he couldn't make a living. He moved to St. Louis, got a job in real estate, and failed at that. He got another job, and was fired. Finally his brothers gave him a job in a store they owned in Galena, Illinois. His salary was $50 a month. His family and his friends considered him a failure.

When the Civil War began in 1861, the North desperately needed trained officers. Grant was appointed a colonel in the army and rose to be a general. In March, 1864, President Lincoln put him in command of all Northern armies.

Most military men now think Grant was a good general, but not a great one. He had a kind of bulldog quality. He saw clearly what he wanted, and went for it, and kept on until he got it. The Union Armies had more men and more equipment than the Confederates, and Grant used these advantages like a hammer. Men who did not like Grant called him "The Butcher" because of the heavy losses his forces took. But he won victories. Several times Congressmen asked Lincoln to fire Grant. "I can't spare this man," Lincoln told them. "He fights."

Grant's victories brought an end to the Civil War and made him a national hero. The Republicans nominated him for President in 1868. He had never been interested in politics. He had never even voted for President but once in his life. But he was elected easily.

The big problem facing the nation was the reconstruction of the South. As a general, Grant had given the Southern Army very generous terms of surrender. But as President he left the South to Congress. And Congress, under the control of men called Radical Republicans, passed one harsh law after another against the South. When necessary, Grant ordered troops to enforce these laws. But he did not seem to care personally whether the laws were good or bad.

Certainly Grant wanted to be a good President. He settled a quarrel with Great Britain that had started during the Civil War. He helped set up Yellowstone National Park, the first national park in the country. But often he seemed to know very little of what was going on around him.

Outside the army, Grant proved to be a very poor judge of men. Many of those he appointed to office turned out to be crooks and thieves. Completely honest himself, he could not see what was happening. Even when he was told, he would not believe it.

By the end of his first term there were a number of people in his own party who thought Grant should not be reelected. However, they could not agree on another candidate. Grant himself was still popular with the nation. And the happy crooks in his party wanted to keep him. He was reelected by a large majority.

The scandals continued. Laws passed by Congress and enforced by Union soldiers had established crooked State Governments in the South. In the North, railroads and whiskey manufacturers bribed government officials. Other officials used political jobs to make dishonest money from the Post Office and from government business. Many of these officials had been appointed by President Grant. Often they were his personal friends.

Still, everyone knew Grant himself was honest. When his second term ended he was still popular. He made a round-the-world tour. He was met with honors wherever he went. He came home and bought a large house in New York City.

Now he needed more money and he invested everything he had in a banking business. Then he left the management of the business up to "friends." He still trusted his friends. But these friends were like some he had appointed to political office. The business went bankrupt. Suddenly Grant was not only without money, but deeply in debt.

About this same time Grant, who had always been a heavy smoker, learned that he had cancer of the throat.

Grant could have lived out his time on charity. He did not want that. He wanted to pay off his debts and leave something for his family. A publisher offered him money if he would write the story of his life. Grant went to work although he knew he was dying. He was in pain much of the time. But courage was one thing the old soldier always had in plenty. Four days before his death he finished the autobiography. It not only made a fortune for his family, it turned out to be a very good and honest book.

Rutherford Hayes

19th President of the United States 1877-1881

Born: October 4, 1822, at Delaware, Ohio.
Died: January 17, 1893, at Fremont, Ohio.

Rutherford Hayes' father owned a store in Delaware, Ohio. Rutherford was a serious, hard-working boy. In grade school he was the champion speller. Later he graduated at the top of his class from Kenyon College, then went to Harvard Law School.

When Hayes first opened his law office in Cincinnati he had very few clients. To save money he slept in his office. But not for long. He won several big cases and soon he had all the work he could handle.

When the Civil War began Hayes was appointed a captain of volunteers. He had no military training, but he proved to be a very dashing officer. He was wounded four times and had four horses killed under him. Before the war was over he was a Major General.

Hayes was still in the army when the Republican Party asked him to run for Congress. He refused to go home and campaign. Any officer who left his post to run for political office, Hayes said, "ought to be scalped." He was elected anyway, but stayed with the army until the war was over.

Hayes served two terms in Congress, then was elected Governor of Ohio. As Governor he helped get Negroes the right to vote. He helped start Ohio State University. He worked hard to improve the Civil Service and make the State Government more honest. In fact, he ran such a strict government that some of the unhappy politicians in his own party began to call him "Old Granny."

As the Presidential election of 1876 drew near, most persons thought the Democrats were sure to win. The Republican Administration under Grant was in disgrace. The party itself was divided. Some hoped they could keep on just as they were. Others thought the only chance to win was to have a candidate known for his honesty. This group nominated Rutherford B. Hayes.

The Democratic candidate was named Samuel J. Tilden. When the election was over Tilden had 4,284,020 votes. Hayes had 4,036,572 votes. These were popular votes—the votes of individual people all over the country. But it was the electoral college that cast the final vote. Here 185 votes were needed to win. Tilden had 184. And the votes of four states were contested. Both the Democrats and Republicans claimed them. Three of these states—Florida, South Carolina and Louisiana—were in the South. Although the Civil War had been over for three years, there was still a great deal of argument over who could vote and who couldn't. Both the Democrats and the Republicans claimed to have won. Both sent electors to Washington.

If Tilden got one single vote from any of these states, he would win the election. But if Hayes got every vote, he would win.

In Congress the argument went on for months. The time for the new President to take office came closer and closer. And still nobody knew who the new President would be.

Finally a deal was made. The Democrats agreed to accept a decision made by a committee—and for the committee to have eight Republicans and seven Democrats. Quite naturally, the committee voted eight to seven to give all the votes from all the contested states to the Republicans. This made Rutherford B. Hayes President.

In return, the Republicans promised that Federal troops would be withdrawn from the South.

President Hayes kept the promise. On April 24, 1877, the last Federal troops left Louisiana. The long bloody period known as the Reconstruction Era was over.

Hayes tried hard to run an honest administration. He appointed honest men to office. He tried to get rid of some of the crooks. He ordered that no government employee should take part in politics.

Many of the professional politicians in Hayes' own party did not like some of the reforms he tried to make. Congress would not pass some of the laws he wanted for honest government. Some laws that he did not want were passed by Congress over his veto.

Because of Congress, President Hayes did not make all the reforms he would have liked. But on the whole he left the Federal Government more honest than he found it. He refused to run for a second term and went back to his home in Ohio. There he died on January 17, 1893.

James Garfield

20th President of the United States 1881

Born: November 19, 1831, at Orange, Ohio.
Died: September 19, 1881, at Elberon, New Jersey.

James Garfield's father was a farmer in Cuyahoga County, Ohio. He died before James was two years old and the child was raised by his mother and older brother. They were very poor and there was little chance to go to school.

But James Garfield decided that he wanted an education. He began to go to school wherever and whenever he could. He worked at any kind of odd job that would leave him time for his books. He learned rapidly. Soon one of his favorite tricks was to write Latin with one hand and Greek with the other at the same time. Before Garfield was 30 years old he was president of a small college.

By this time the whole nation was becoming more and more worried about the problem of slavery. Garfield believed slavery was immoral. He began to make speeches against letting the western territories become slave states.

When the Civil War began Garfield raised a regiment of volunteer soldiers. Many of the young men had been his students.

Garfield had no military training, but he knew how to learn. He studied everything he could find on military tactics. He became an excellent officer. When he was 31 he was made the youngest Brigadier General in the army.

Garfield was also elected to Congress from Ohio. At first he refused to leave the army. Finally President Lincoln talked him into quitting the army and taking his seat in Congress.

For the next 18 years Garfield served in Congress. During much of this time the American people did not demand very honest government from their representatives in Congress. As a result, they did not get very honest government. Many politicians came to believe the purpose of government was to make the politicians and their friends rich. This was especially true during the administration of President Grant.

As a Congressman, Garfield was accused of taking bribes. He denied the charges, and they were never proved. Probably Garfield was not as bad as, and maybe not much better than, the average Congressman of his time.

In 1880 the Republican Party had three well-known candidates for President. But at the nominating convention no one of them could get a majority. Finally Garfield was named as a compromise.

During the campaign the Democrats talked a lot about the bribes Garfield was said to have taken in Congress. But they could not prove anything and Garfield won an easy victory.

Had Garfield lived he might have developed into a good President. He began by fighting some of the powerful Congressmen who wanted to run the government their way. He was going to prove, Garfield said, that the President was not just a clerk for Congress.

The Federal Government had almost no civil service. Several Presidents had asked Congress for good civil service laws, but Congress would not pass them. With every new administration many government workers got fired and new ones hired, who had voted for the administration. Each new President had to spend much of his time handing out jobs.

This was true with President Garfield. Then on July 2, 1881, he was shot by a man he had refused to give a job.

The entire nation was shocked. As a result of the President's murder people began to demand more honest government. They demanded better civil service laws that would keep honest government workers on the job. And because the people demanded it, Congress finally did improve the civil service laws.

Chester Arthur

21st President of the United States 1881-1885

Born: October 5, 1830, at Fairfield, Vermont.
Died: November 18, 1886, at New York City.

Chester Arthur's career showed that sometimes the office of President may work a small miracle in the man who holds it.

As a young man, Arthur taught school, then became a lawyer. He was interested in politics, but he did not run for office himself. Instead he worked with political "Bosses." These were men who tried to control elections by giving jobs and money to people who would vote as the Bosses wished. In time Arthur became an important political Boss himself.

After the Civil War, President Grant appointed Arthur the Collector of the Port of New York. This was a very important political position. Arthur used it to give jobs to people who would vote and work for the Republican Party. Then people had to give back part of their pay to the Republican Party. They also had to vote the way they were told.

Chester Arthur was not the only person doing this sort of thing. Indeed, it was a rather common practice under President Grant. Arthur himself did not believe it was wrong. He was a friendly, good humored man, always very polite. People called him the "Gentleman Boss."

After Grant's second term Rutherford Hayes became President. Hayes said that men who held important government jobs should not take part in the management of political parties. Arthur refused to obey. He seemed to believe that his first duty was to his party, not to his country. As a result, President Hayes forced him out of his job.

In 1880 the Republican Party was split in two groups. One group, called the Stalwarts, wanted to nominate Ulysses S. Grant for a third term as President. The other group wanted a candidate who would insist on reform and more honest government.

Chester Arthur was a Stalwart. He worked hard to have Grant nominated. Finally, however, James Garfield won the nomination. As a compromise, Arthur himself was nominated for Vice President. He and Garfield won the election.

As President, Garfield wanted to reform the civil service. He thought

people should have to take a written examination in order to get a government job. Then the jobs would go to those who were best qualified, not just to those who voted for this or that political party. Vice President Arthur was openly opposed. He wanted things left as they were.

Garfield had been in office only a few months when he was murdered by a man named Charles Giteau. When he shot the President, Giteau shouted, "I am a Stalwart! Arthur is now President!" Later Giteau said he had killed the President because Garfield had refused to give him a job.

The entire nation was shocked at the President's murder, and at the reason for it. Many people were frightened. They wondered what sort of President Arthur would make. Some Stalwart politicians were happy to have Arthur become President. They thought things would go back to the way they had been under President Grant.

Everybody was in for a surprise.

Arthur could not forget that Garfield had been murdered by a man who shouted, "Arthur is now President!" He could not forget that it was the kind of politics he and other Stalwarts had stood for that caused such a thing to happen. A change came over Chester Arthur. He realized that as President, his duty was to all the people, not just to one party. The very size of his job made him feel humble. He tried to carry on Garfield's work and asked Congress for a new civil service law.

The old Stalwart politicians became angry at Arthur. But now the people themselves were demanding reform. In the next Congressional election many of the old politicians were defeated. After that it did not take long to get the new law passed.

Arthur went on to work hard and honestly at being President. He helped bring the navy up to date with modern ships. He changed the postal system to give better and cheaper service. But the Stalwart politicians did not forgive him. They refused to nominate him for President in 1884.

Arthur went back to his home in New York. He would never be elected President on his own. But the people of the country admired him far more than they had a few years before.

Grover Cleveland

22nd President of the United States 1885-1889
24th President of the United States 1893-1897

Born: March 18, 1837, at Caldwell, New Jersey.
Died: June 24, 1908, at Princeton, New Jersey.

Grover Cleveland's father was a Presbyterian minister with a big family and little money. When Grover was 14 he had to quit school to work in a store. At 17 he left home to look for a better job. He planned to go to Cleveland, Ohio, because he liked the name. On the way he stopped to visit an uncle in Buffalo, New York. There he got a job in a lawyer's office making $4.00 a week. But he also had a chance to study. By the time he was 22 he was a lawyer.

Cleveland's father had died and his mother was poor. When the Civil War started in 1861, Grover and his two brothers drew lots. Two of them would join the army, they decided; the other brother would stay at home to support their mother. Grover drew the short straw and kept working. Later his political enemies would say he stayed out of the army because he was afraid. No one who really knew Grover Cleveland ever believed it.

Cleveland became a very successful lawyer. In 1881 he was asked by the Democratic Party to run for mayor of Buffalo. Most of the people in the city were Republicans, but many of them were unhappy with the present administration. They wanted a change and a more honest government.

Cleveland was elected. He gave the people an even more honest government than some of them wanted. He reorganized the city so that it ran more cheaply. He fired anybody he caught taking graft. Within one year he had cleaned up the city and the people elected him Governor of New York.

As Governor, Grover Cleveland made sure the state got its money's worth for every dollar spent. Some of the politicians did not like it, but the people did.

In 1884 Cleveland was nominated by the Democrats to run for President. No Democrat had been elected President since the Civil War. However, at this time the Republican Party was split in two groups. One group, called "Mugwumps," were demanding reform and

a more honest government. Because they did not like the Republican candidate, they voted for Cleveland. It was a very close election, but Cleveland won.

Cleveland began to reform the Federal Government as he had the State Government of New York. He improved the civil service to get better government workers. He forced the railroads to return 81,000,000 acres of government land they had taken illegally. He made sure the navy got the best ships possible for the least money.

No President has ever worked harder than Cleveland. Often he was at his desk until two and three o'clock in the morning. He studied every bill Congress passed and vetoed more than 400 of them. Many of these gave pensions to Civil War veterans whether or not they had been wounded. Cleveland believed this was dishonest. When one politician told him his actions might keep him from being reelected he said, "What's the use of being elected or reelected unless you stand for something?"

One of the big problems facing the country in 1888 was the tariff. This is a tax paid on products brought into the United States from other countries. The higher the tariff, the higher the price for which these products had to be sold in this country. American manufacturers and the people who worked for them wanted a high tariff. This allowed the American manufacturer to sell his own product at a high price too. Farmers and other people wanted a low tariff so they could buy goods cheaply.

In the election of 1888 Cleveland and the Democratic Party stood for a low tariff. It was a very close election. Cleveland got more popular votes than Harrison. But Harrison won in the electoral college and became President.

When Mrs. Cleveland moved out of the White House she told the servants to take good care of it. "I want everything just the way it is now when we come back," she said. "That will be exactly four years from now."

She was right. In 1892 Cleveland and Harrison once more ran against each other. This time Cleveland won. He was the only President in U.S. history to serve two terms that did not directly follow one another.

Cleveland's second term was much like his first. He worked hard. He did what he thought was right, whether it was popular or not. When a railroad strike in Chicago interfered with the mail, Cleveland sent Federal troops. He broke up the strike. "If it takes the entire army and navy to deliver one post card in Chicago," he said, "that card will be delivered." A serious depression swept the country. Cleveland tried to improve the Treasury system rather than help the people who were out of work. His methods were not very successful. But he thought it would not be constitutional for the Federal Government to help individual people or businesses.

Cleveland's second term ended in 1897. He left the Federal Government a better working and more honest organization than he found it. His last words before he died were: "I have tried so hard to do right."

Benjamin Harrison

23rd President of the United States 1889-1893

Born: August 20, 1833, near North Bend, Ohio.
Died: March 13, 1901, at Indianapolis, Indiana.

As a boy Benjamin Harrison spent most of his time on a farm owned by his father. He always liked to read. He was a good student. By the time he was 21 years old he had graduated from college and married. With his bride he moved to Indianapolis, Indiana, to practice law. He was quickly successful.

When the Civil War began Benjamin Harrison formed a regiment of volunteers. He was appointed Colonel. His regiment took part in many battles and Harrison proved to be a brave and good officer. After the war he went back to Indianapolis to practise law.

In January, 1881, Harrison was elected to the U.S. Senate. Because his father had been a Congressman and his grandfather had been President, Harrison's name was already well known throughout the country. It was partly for this reason that in 1888 the Republicans nominated him for President.

Harrison was a small man, only five feet six inches tall. During the Civil War his soldiers had affectionately called him Little Ben. Now the Democrats used the name to imply that he was not "big" enough to be President. In turn, the Republican sang a song called "Grandfather's Hat Fits Ben." Cartoonists drew pictures of him as a very little man almost hidden under a huge, high-topped hat.

Harrison had the ability to think about only one subject at a time. Sometimes, deep in thought, he would walk right past people he knew without recognizing them. Because of this some people said he was cold and unfriendly. Actually he was a warm, kind-hearted man. But he was not a good "back slapping" politician. He did not like to meet big crowds of strangers. So he ran what was called a "front porch" campaign. He stayed at home and talked with the politicians who came to see him in small groups.

It was a very close race for President. Actually Grover Cleveland, the Democrat, got more popular votes than Harrison. But in the electoral college Harrison won 233 to 168.

As President, Harrison wanted to continue the reform of the civil service started by Cleveland. He appointed a vigorous, hard-working young man named Theodore Roosevelt as commissioner. But not even Roosevelt could do much with this Congress that did not want reform. Within one year 30,000 postmasters were fired so new ones, who had friends in Congress, could be appointed.

Harrison was in favor of a high tariff. With his help Congress passed the McKinley Tariff Act. This put a high tax on goods shipped to the United States from other countries. As a result, prices went up. Farmers and small business men complained. At the same time some of the big manufacturers were having labor troubles. Labor unions said that the power of the government was being used to help the rich and hurt the poor. Many voters turned against Harrison and he was defeated for reelection in 1892.

Harrison went back to his home in Indianapolis. He wrote books about United States government and continued to practice law until his death in 1901.

William McKinley

25th President of the United States 1897-1901

Born: January 27, 1843, at Niles, Ohio.
Died: September 14, 1901, at Buffalo, New York.

William McKinley was born in Niles, Ohio, a town with a population of about 300. When he was nine years old the family moved to Poland, Ohio, which wasn't much bigger. McKinley went to local schools, then to Allegheny College. He had been in college only a short time when he became sick and had to go home.

The Civil War had just begun. McKinley joined the army as a private. He was the first person to volunteer from his home town. Before the war was over he was promoted to major.

After the war, McKinley studied law. He began to practice in Canton, Ohio, and married the daughter of the local banker. McKinley was a pale, dignified, pleasant man. And very smart. He knew from the first what he wanted and he aimed for it. Later he told friends, "I have never been in doubt since I was old enough to think intelligently that I would some day be made President."

He started by running for Congress. He served there for 14 years and became one of the leaders of the Republican Party. In 1891 he was elected Governor of Ohio. He made a national reputation as a businesslike executive. Then in 1898 he was nominated for President.

McKinley ran what was called a "front porch" campaign. It was something like the campaign of President Benjamin Harrison but for a different reason. Mrs. McKinley was an invalid. Her husband was devoted to her. He refused to leave her to travel around the country for long periods of time. So the wealthy men who were backing McKinley brought people from all over the country to see him. McKinley stood on his front porch and talked to them.

The Democrats claimed McKinley would have to take orders from the rich bankers in the big cities. But he won the election by a large majority.

At this time Cuba still belonged to Spain. For several years the Cubans had been fighting for their independence. Many people in the United States wanted to help them. Some newspapers were particularly anxious for the U.S. to declare war on Spain. They printed

stories about how the Spanish mistreated the Cubans. Not all of these stories were true, but they made people angry.

McKinley did not want war. He knew that Spain had finally agreed to give Cuba its independence without fighting. But he gave in to the newspapers and asked Congress for war with Spain.

Within a few months American soldiers had defeated the Spanish in Cuba. In Manila Bay an American fleet destroyed the Spanish fleet.

And in about one hundred days the war was over. The United States took over the Philippines, the islands of Guam and Puerto Rico. Cuba was given its independence.

Even before this war with Spain there were people who wanted the United States to take over the Hawaiian Islands. Americans living in the islands had staged a revolution and overthrown the old Hawaiian Government. They wanted to become part of the United States so that they could sell sugar grown in the islands for a high price. President Cleveland had refused to recognize the new Hawaiian Government. He said it had been forced on the people against their will. President McKinley was not as particular. At his request Congress quickly voted to annex the islands. On July 7, 1898, Hawaii became an American territory.

In 1900 McKinley was elected to a second term. All over the country business was good. In 1901 Buffalo, New York, put on a big fair. McKinley visited it on September 6. In one of the buildings he was shaking hands with a huge crowd of people. One of these was a little girl. President McKinley took the flower he wore on his coat and gave it to her. Then a man stepped up as if to shake hands. He had a handkerchief wrapped around his right hand. Inside the handkerchief was a gun. He fired two shots into the President. The man's name was Leon Czolgosz. He said he did not believe in government and wanted to kill a great ruler.

Even as President McKinley lay wounded he thought of his invalid wife. He whispered to a friend beside him, "Be careful how you tell her. Oh, be careful how you tell her."

Eight days later he died.

Theodore Roosevelt

26th President of the United States 1901-1909

Born: October 27, 1858, at New York City.
Died: January 6, 1919, at Sagamore Hill, Long Island, New York.

Even as a child, Theodore Roosevelt had to wear glasses. He suffered with asthma. He was sick much of the time, but he determined to build a healthy body. He took endless exercise. He ran and swam and lifted weights. Slowly he overcame his asthma. He developed a deep chest, powerful arms and shoulders, and great endurance.

As a boy Roosevelt never went to a regular school. Because of his poor health, he had private tutors. At 18 he entered Harvard University. He made fair grades, graduated at 22, and got married the same year.

Roosevelt's wealthy friends told him not to go into politics because it was "a dirty business." Roosevelt's answer was that it didn't have to be dirty. A man could be a politician and work honestly for the welfare of his country. He joined a Republican club and at 23 was elected to the State Legislature. Within six weeks he was trying to get a crooked judge thrown out of office. He didn't succeed, but he made a reputation as a fearless and honest legislator.

In 1884 Roosevelt's young wife and his mother both died within a few hours of one another. To forget his grief, Roosevelt moved to the Dakota Territory. He bought a ranch and for two years he worked as a cowboy. He spent long days in the saddle. He even became a deputy sheriff and helped hunt down several outlaws. Soon he had the reputation of being as fearless on the frontier as in the legislature. Later he said, "There were all kinds of things of which I was afraid at first . . . from grizzly bears to 'mean' horses and gunfighters; but by acting as if I were not afraid I gradually ceased to be afraid."

After two years Roosevelt went back east. He married again. He served in Washington on the Civil Service Commission, and in New York City as Commissioner of Police. In 1897 President McKinley appointed him Assistant Secretary of the Navy.

At this time Cuba was fighting to become independent of Spain. Roosevelt wanted the United States to join in. He said President McKinley was "lily livered" for not asking Congress to declare war on Spain.

When war was finally declared, Roosevelt quit his government job. He had always been a little ashamed that his own father had not fought in the Civil War. Now he formed a cavalry regiment called the Rough Riders. In it were wealthy college athletes from the east and hard riding cowboys from the west. In Cuba Roosevelt led them in a charge up San Juan Hill to capture a Spanish fort. Years later he would say, "San Juan was the greatest day of my life."

After the Spanish-American War, Roosevelt was elected Governor of New York. He was a strong governor, and an honest one. Many of the professional politicians were afraid of him. It was for this reason that in 1900 they nominated him for Vice President. They thought that as Vice President he would be out of the way with little to do. But on September 6, 1901, President McKinley was shot. Roosevelt was mountain-climbing, but he rushed back to take the oath of office as President.

"Now look," one of his enemies moaned, "that damned cowboy is President of the United States."

Roosevelt was 43, the youngest man ever to be President. And certainly he was one of the most colorful. He was a showman. His favorite word was "bully!" which meant "wonderful." Whatever Teddy Roosevelt did, he had a bully time doing it. And being President was bulliest of all.

At the same time, Roosevelt was completely sincere about his work. With all his heart he believed in a strong and unified country. But during the Presidential election he had seen that the nation was in danger of breaking up. The division now was not between North and South, but between the rich and the poor. At that time, the rich were very rich indeed, and the poor were very poor. The average working man could earn only between $400 and $500 a year. At the same time many big businesses were joining to form "trusts." The trusts could kill off any competition. They could force men to work for them at low wages, or not work at all.

Roosevelt was proud of the things American big business could produce. But he saw that small businesses and working men needed protection. People called him a "trust buster." Roosevelt said he did not want to "bust the trusts" but only to control them. He wanted everybody to have a "square deal." Because of this his administration became known as the Square Deal. He forced the railroads to give fair rates to small business. He forced the owners of coal mines to pay better wages. He forced Congress to pass laws protecting the people from impure food and drugs.

Many of the professional politicians did not like Roosevelt, but the people did. In 1904 he was reelected by a huge majority.

No President has done more to save the natural resources of the country for the people than Theodore Roosevelt. He established national parks and more than 125 million acres as national forests.

Roosevelt believed in a strong navy. He got Congress to build new battleships and cruisers. In international affairs, Roosevelt said, the President should "speak softly and carry a big stick." Roosevelt's own "big stick" was a powerful navy. He sent it on a cruise around the world to show American strength.

Roosevelt also wanted a canal across the Isthmus of Panama. The canal would allow the Navy to move rapidly from one ocean to the other. At this time the isthmus belonged to Columbia. Roosevelt tried to buy the land for the canal, but the Columbian Government hesitated to sell.

Some of the business men in the isthmus who wanted the canal began to plot a revolution. They had the help of U.S. Army officers. Roosevelt also knew about the plan. He sent his warships to the area. When the revolution started, American sailors stopped the Columbian Government from sending troops to put down the revolution. Two days later the United States recognized the new Republic of Panama. Then the new country leased part of its land to the United States for the canal.

Later, enemies of Roosevelt would say he had actually caused the revolution in Panama. The truth is, he did not cause it; but he certainly helped it along to get what he wanted. Roosevelt said he was more proud of the Panama Canal than of anything else done during his administration. He refused to run for a third term. Instead he went big game hunting in Africa. He toured Europe. He wrote books and made speeches. Still, it was not quite enough to keep him busy. He was unhappy with the way the new President, Taft, was running the country, and in 1912 he once more ran for President. Since Taft was the Republican candidate, Roosevelt formed a new party, called the Progressive Party.

While in Milwaukee to make a campaign speech, Roosevelt was shot

by an insane man. He was only wounded and finished his speech before going to the hospital. When a reporter asked how he felt, Roosevelt said, "I feel as strong as a bull moose." From that time on his party was known as the "Bull Moose Party."

In this election the Republican vote was split between Taft and Roosevelt. The Democratic candidate, Woodrow Wilson, was elected.

Roosevelt went back to his home on Long Island. He wrote his autobiography. He wrote magazine articles. He went to South America and spent months exploring an unknown river called the River of Doubt. He got a jungle fever and almost died.

By now he was blind in one eye. He would never be really well again. But when World War I started he wanted to raise a regiment and go to France to fight. President Wilson refused. He wanted the war run by professional military men—and Roosevelt never forgave him.

Less than two years later Roosevelt died quietly in his sleep. It was one of the few things he ever did quietly.

William Taft

27th President of the United States 1909-1913

Born: September 15, 1857, at Cincinnati, Ohio.
Died: March 8, 1930, at Washington, D.C.

Even as a boy William Taft was big. His brothers and sisters called him "Big Lub." Other people called him Big Bill. He grew to be about six feet tall and weighed close to 300 pounds. Only a little of it was fat. He was a good tennis player and an excellent dancer. He liked to ride horseback, if he had a horse that could carry him.

Taft's father was a successful lawyer, active in Republican politics. His wife's father had been the law partner of President Rutherford B. Hayes. Their friends urged Big Bill Taft to go into politics, but he was more interested in law. He was a good lawyer. In 1887 the Governor of Ohio appointed Taft to the State Supreme Court. He liked being a judge. The next year he ran for the same office and was elected.

In 1901 Taft was appointed Civil Governor of the Philippines, which then belonged to the United States. He made a good governor. He liked the Filipinos, and they liked him. Then in 1904 President Theodore Roosevelt appointed Taft Secretary of War. He did an excellent job. Roosevelt was often away, but everything was all right in Washington, Roosevelt said, because Big Bill Taft was "sitting on the lid."

Roosevelt admired Taft's ability. It was largely because of Roosevelt that the Republican Party nominated Taft for President in 1908. Taft, however, was not happy about the idea. He didn't think he would make a good President. His ambition was to be appointed to the Supreme Court. But Mrs. Taft wanted to be First Lady. She talked Taft into running for President. With Roosevelt's backing, he was elected.

Taft planned to carry out Roosevelt's progressive policies. And actually he did a pretty good job of it. He improved the civil service. He was the first President to put aside government-owned lands where oil and coal had been found. He said the profit from these should belong to the people, not to private business.

But Taft simply could not do things with Roosevelt's flair and flash. Roosevelt and many of his followers began to think Taft was not doing enough. Taft himself believed that the powers of the President should be limited. He did not believe that a President, even in a good cause,

should take over powers normally given to Congress. He kept framed on his desk a saying by Lincoln: "I do the very best I know how—the very best I can; and I mean to keep on doing so until the end."

Roosevelt and his friends said that Taft had sold out Roosevelt's ideals. When the Republicans nominated Taft to run for a second term in 1912, Roosevelt formed the Bull Moose Party to run against him. The Democrats nominated Woodrow Wilson.

Taft was deeply hurt by the things Roosevelt said about him. And he had never liked to campaign. He knew that in a three-way race against Wilson and Roosevelt he had no chance. But he had been nominated, and he did his best.

In the election Roosevelt got more votes than Taft. But Wilson got more than either of them and was elected.

Taft had been one of the most unhappy Presidents. When he left the White House, he said: "I am glad to be going. This is the lonesomest place in the world." He went back to his law practice. He taught law at Yale. Then in 1921 he was appointed Chief Justice of the U.S. Supreme Court. This was the work he loved. He served until his retirement because of ill health in 1930. "I don't even remember that I ever was President," he said happily.

Woodrow Wilson

28th President of the United States 1913-1921

Born: December 28, 1856, at Staunton, Virginia.
Died: February 3, 1924, at Washington, D.C.

Woodrow Wilson was born in Virginia five years before the start of the Civil War. His father and grandfather were Presbyterian preachers. At one time his father's church was turned into a hospital for wounded Confederate soldiers. All his life Wilson was proud of the gallant fight the South had made. At the same time, he was glad the North won and kept the Union undivided.

With his family and close friends, Wilson was warm, witty and

loving. To many other persons he seemed cold and even bitter. He often told people what he thought was wrong with them, and turned his friends into enemies.

Wilson had a high forehead, a long, thin nose, and a firm mouth. He looked like a teacher or a preacher. He was not a big man, but he was lean and strong. At Princeton he played football and later he helped coach the team. He took a law degree and for a little while practiced law in Atlanta, Georgia. But he did not like law. He went back to school, took a Ph.D. degree and began to teach. In 1902 he was made President of Princeton University.

At Princeton Wilson wanted to do away with the "eating clubs." These were small social groups and Wilson did not think they were democratic. He wanted to change Princeton, he said, from "a place where there are youngsters doing tasks to a place where there are men thinking." Not all his reforms were accepted, but it made Wilson known as a man who believed in honest, democratic government. In 1910 he was elected Governor of New Jersey. Two years later he was elected President.

Like Theodore Roosevelt, Wilson believed the job of the President was to represent all the people. Congressmen, he said, represented special areas and groups. There was no one but the President "to look out for the general interests of the whole country."

Wilson got Congress to lower the tariff. This angered some big manufacturers, but it brought lower prices to the public. He reformed the national banking system. He got Congress to declare it was not against Federal law for working men to go on strike, as some big businesses had claimed it was.

Wilson had been in office less than two years when World War I began in Europe. It was Wilson's great hope that the United States could stay out. He tried to find ways to help the countries that were fighting to make peace.

In 1916 Wilson was nominated for a second term. During the campaign one of the slogans was "He kept us out of war." It helped Wilson win reelection. But soon German submarines began to sink American ships without warning. Many lives were lost.

Wilson finally asked Congress to declare war against Germany.

Wilson hoped with all his heart that this was "a war to end war." Even while the fighting was going on he drew up a famous "Fourteen Points" peace plan. The most important point called for a League of Nations. Wilson hoped that such a League could settle all future arguments between nations.

In November, 1918, Germany surrendered and the fighting in Europe stopped. The League of Nations was soon formed. But the United States could not join unless the U.S. Senate approved.

Some Senators did not want the United States to join at all. Many others wanted to join, but only if certain changes were made in the League plan. If Wilson had agreed to the changes, the Senate would have passed the bill. But Wilson refused to make any compromise. Instead, he started on a trip around the country making speeches in favor of the League.

For many months he had been working long hours, day and night, under great strain. Now, suddenly, he became too sick to go on. He had a stroke that paralyzed his left side. For two months he was hardly conscious. No one except his doctor, his secretary and his family could see him.

Without Wilson's leadership the U.S. Senate voted against joining the League of Nations. And without the United States, the League was of little value.

Gradually Wilson recovered some of his strength. But he was never really well again. After his term in office he took no more part in politics. But other men would continue to fight for his ideals and the hope of a world without war.

Warren Harding

29th President of the United States 1921-1923

Born: November 2, 1865, at Blooming Grove, Ohio.
Died: August 2, 1923, at San Francisco.

Warren Harding was raised in small Ohio towns. He was a tall, handsome, bright boy. Everybody liked him. He quit school at 17, taught briefly in a country school, and got a job on a weekly newspaper called the Marion, Ohio, *Democratic Mirror*. A year or so later he and two friends bought a bankrupt weekly paper called the *Star*.

The town of Marion was growing, and the paper grew with it. Harding married the daughter of the local banker. He made money.

A few years later he ran for Governor and was defeated. But in 1914 he was elected to the United States Senate.

Harding liked being a Senator. He didn't worry too much about the big national problems. He was a loyal Republican and usually he voted the way he was told. He was also loyal to his friends back home. He spent most of his time trying to find jobs for them. He was so busy at this he missed half the roll calls in the Senate.

One of Harding's friends was a politician named Harry Daugherty. Daugherty set out to see if he could get Harding elected President.

At the Republican convention in 1920 the three important candidates split the votes between them. No one of them could get enough votes to be nominated. So a number of powerful politicians met Harry Daugherty in "a smoke filled room" in a local hotel. They all knew Harding. They liked him; everybody liked him.

At two o'clock in the morning they agreed to support Harding.

World War I had been over for only two years. The American people were weary of war-time problems and shortages. They blamed Europe for the war, and they wanted no more to do with it.

Harding promised a "return to normalcy." He won the election in a landslide.

As President, Harding wanted to do something for world peace. He called a disarmament conference in Washington. There Charles Hughes, the Secretary of State, worked out a plan for limiting the world's navies. This was probably the most important action in Harding's administration.

Unfortunately, not all the men Harding appointed were either

honest or capable. He made Harry Daugherty Attorney General. And he brought in so many of his old Ohio pals that in Washington they became known as the Ohio Gang. Some of these men had little ability. Others were outright crooks. They set out to get rich off the government.

No one can be sure just how much Harding knew about what his friends were doing. He must have had some idea. But he did nothing about it.

Then, in August, 1923, he suddenly became ill. A few days later he died.

Then the stories began to come out. Some members of the Ohio Gang committed suicide rather than face trial. Some, including the Secretary of Interior, went to jail. And as the people learned about how crooked Harding's administration had been, they began to wonder about the President's sudden illness and death. Soon rumors said he had killed himself. Other rumors said his wife had poisoned him. The exact truth was never known. But now it seems probable that he died of a heart attack.

Calvin Coolidge

30th President of the United States 1923-1929

Born: July 4, 1872, at Plymouth Notch, Vermont.
Died: January 5, 1933, at Northampton, Mass.

Calvin Coolidge was raised in Vermont where his father had a country store and small farm. He graduated from Amherst College and began to practice law in Northampton, Massachusetts. He went into politics and was elected to the State Legislature. He came back to Northampton to be mayor. He was Lieutenant Governor in 1916, Governor in 1918.

Calvin Coolidge was not a typical, back-slapping politician. He had a lean, sour look. His mouth turned down at the corners. It shut as tight as a clam shell, and he didn't open it any more than he needed to. When he made speeches they were short and to the point. He became known as "Silent Cal."

Coolidge worked hard. He gave people the impression of being safe,

conservative, and totally honest. Each time he ran for office he got more votes than the time before.

While Coolidge was Governor of Massachusetts, he first drew national attention. In 1919 the police in Boston went on strike. Coolidge promptly called out the entire National Guard and broke the strike. "There is no right to strike against the public safety by anybody, anywhere, at any time," he said. Largely because of this action, he was nominated by the Republicans for Vice President in 1920. He was elected with President Harding.

When Harding died suddenly in 1923, Coolidge was visiting his father. He was awakened by a messenger in the middle of the night and told that he was now President. By the light of a kerosene lamp, his hand on the old family Bible, Calvin Coolidge took the oath of office from his father, who was justice of the peace.

The scandals of the Harding administration were not yet public. When they did become known, they did not bother Coolidge. Even the Democrats never suspected Coolidge of being dishonest.

Coolidge said that "The business of America is business." And the business of government was to keep out of business. "When things are going all right," he said, "it is a good plan to let them alone."

Things seemed to be going very well indeed. Business was booming.

People were gambling on the stock market, and stocks were going up. Prices were going up. Wages were going up. And Coolidge was tremendously popular. He made people feel safe. He never gambled a nickle, and never spent a nickle that he didn't have to. He is probably the only President who ever saved money from his salary.

He did not talk any more as President than he had before. Once a young lady sitting next to him at a White House dinner said, "Mr. President, I have made a bet I can get more than three words out of you during the meal."

Without even looking at her he said, "You lose."

In 1924 Coolidge was elected President in his own right. Probably he could have been elected again in 1928. But he said, "I do not choose to run." Some historians believe he did not really mean it, but the voters did. At the end of his term he retired.

This was lucky for Coolidge. Around the country a few people had been saying that unless something was done to slow down the boom, it was sure to break and bring on a depression. Coolidge did not believe them. He took no action.

A few months later the boom did break. The country was plunged into its most terrible depression. Coolidge did not understand. He kept thinking times ought to get better. And instead they got worse. Shortly before his death in 1933 he said, "I no longer fit in with these times."

Herbert Hoover

31st President of the United States 1929-1933

Born: August 10, 1874, at West Branch, Iowa.
Died: October 20, 1964, at New York City.

Herbert Hoover was the first President born west of the Mississippi River. His father, a blacksmith in a small Iowa town, died when Herbert was six. His mother, a deeply religious Quaker, supported her three children by preaching and taking in sewing. She died when Herbert was nine. After that he lived with an uncle in Oregon.

The uncle had a real estate office where Herbert worked after school. One day a man came in who was a mining engineer. Herbert heard him talking about his work and how he traveled from one job to another around the world. The boy was deeply impressed. When he was 17 he went to Stanford University to study engineering.

After graduation Hoover worked in San Francisco. When he was 23 he went to Australia. He helped develop one of the richest gold mines in the world. Two years later he came back to California and married his college sweetheart, Lou Henry.

By the time Hoover was in his thirties he was rich. Then one member of his engineering firm stole a million dollars. Hoover was not responsible, but he did not want other persons to suffer. He ordered his company to pay back the money.

He kept working. In a few years he was once more a millionaire.

Hoover was in London when World War I began. Suddenly many Americans who had been traveling abroad could not get money to go home. Hoover formed an organization that helped over 100,000 Americans return from Europe. Much of the money he paid out of his own pocket.

When the German army captured Belgium, many of the Belgian people were without food. Hoover helped bring food from the U.S.

and get it through the German lines. His work saved millions of people from starving.

When America entered the war, President Wilson appointed Hoover the Food Administrator. His job was to get the American people to save food so it could be sent to the Allies and soldiers in Europe. Hoover had no real power to enforce his rules, but he got the people to save food anyway.

Because of this work, President Harding appointed Hoover Secretary of Commerce. He worked as hard at this job as at all his other jobs. One newspaper wrote that Hoover was "the Secretary of Commerce and the Under Secretary of Everything Else."

In 1928 the Republicans nominated Hoover for President. He had never run for any political office. But most Americans knew and honored the work he had done. He was elected by a huge majority.

Then, almost suddenly, the good times ended. Businesses that had borrowed too much money failed. Men were out of work. Without jobs they could not buy things. So more businesses failed, and put more men out of work. Banks failed and many people lost all they had saved. Hoover was slow to act. A truly kind man, it hurt him to see people hungry. But he felt the government should not interfere with business.

Nobody truly understood what caused the depression. But because people had to blame something, they blamed Hoover. When people lost their jobs they said it was Hoover's fault the government did not do enough to help.

Finally Hoover established an organization to loan government money to businesses in need. Hoover also started some programs to furnish jobs. These helped, but they did not end the depression. And in the election of 1932 Hoover was overwhelmingly defeated.

Hoover went back to private life. At this time he was hated by many people who thought he was to blame for the depression. But gradually people understood that no one person was to blame. Then in 1940 Russia and Finland went to war. Hoover raised great stocks of food to help feed the Finns. After World War II he was named by President Truman to head the Famine Emergency Commission. This Commission sent food to people in countries destroyed by war. Once more Hoover's work helped save millions of lives.

By the time of Hoover's death the Great Depression was largely forgotten. Hoover himself was widely honored for his good works.

Franklin Roosevelt

32nd President of the United States 1933-1945

Born: January 30, 1882, at Hyde Park, New York.
Died: April 12, 1945, at Warm Springs, Georgia.

Franklin Roosevelt was born into a wealthy and well-known family. President Theodore Roosevelt was his fifth cousin. Franklin was also distantly related to 10 other Presidents: Washington, both Adamses, Madison, Van Buren, both Harrisons, Taylor, Grant, and Taft.

As a boy Franklin Roosevelt never went to public schools. An only child, he often traveled with his parents in Europe. He learned foreign languages. He had private tutors. When he was 14 he was sent to Groton, a private school. Later Roosevelt went to Harvard University. He was a tall, lean, good-looking boy. He went out for the football team and the crew. He never made the varsity though he tried. But all his life he was proud of having been editor of the school paper his senior year.

After Harvard, Roosevelt studied law. He married a distant cousin, named Eleanor Roosevelt. Eleanor's father was dead. At the wedding, his cousin, President Teddy Roosevelt, gave the bride away.

Franklin Roosevelt greatly admired his cousin Teddy. Like Teddy, Franklin believed that politics offered a wealthy man a chance to serve his country. But Teddy Roosevelt was a Republican. Franklin's father was a Democrat. So Franklin joined the Democratic Party.

Franklin began his career by running for the New York State Legislature. No one thought he had a chance, because most people in his county were Republicans. Franklin hired a bright red automobile in which to travel and meet the people. To almost everybody's surprise he was elected.

Franklin was delighted when President Wilson appointed him Assistant Secretary of the Navy, a post Teddy Roosevelt had once held. In his new job he worked hard to build a good navy. When World War I began, Roosevelt wanted to quit his job and join the navy as a fighting man. But President Wilson would not let him go. His work as Assistant Secretary was too important.

After the war, Roosevelt was nominated by the Democrats to run for Vice President. He was defeated, but it gave him a chance to meet people all around the country.

Then in 1921, something happened to change the whole course of Franklin Roosevelt's life. Quite suddenly he became ill with polio. For awhile he could move neither his arms nor legs. Slowly, almost by sheer will power, he fought his way back. He regained the use of his hands and arms. He spent long hours swimming and taking exercise. He was never again able to walk without braces on his legs, but he developed very powerful arms and shoulders.

Even while he was sick Roosevelt kept up his interest in politics. In 1924, walking on crutches, he appeared at the Democratic National Convention to nominate Al Smith for President. Smith was defeated, but he persuaded Roosevelt to run for Governor of New York in 1928.

Roosevelt was elected. He was in office when the Great Depression of the 1930's began. All over the country businesses began to fail. Many people were out of work. With no jobs they could not buy new houses or automobiles. So more businesses failed, and more people were put out of work. Banks failed and families lost their savings.

As Governor of New York, Roosevelt used the power of the state to help businesses and people who were out of work. He talked to the people over the radio. He called these talks "fireside chats," and in them he told the people what he was trying to do.

Partly because of these talks, the Democrats nominated Roosevelt for President in 1932. Herbert Hoover, the Republican President, was running for a second term. Many people blamed Hoover for the depression. This was not fair, but it helped Roosevelt to win.

By the time Roosevelt took office the depression had grown still worse. More than 5000 banks had failed. People were not only out of work, but many were hungry. Many had lost their homes.

Roosevelt took action. First he declared a Bank Holiday. This closed all the banks so no more could fail. Then the banks were reopened a few at a time with government help. Roosevelt asked for new laws to help the farmers and small businessmen. He asked for laws to help people about to lose their homes.

Quickly Congress passed the laws Roosevelt asked for. As one Congressman said, "The house is burning down and the President of the United States says this is the way to put out the fire."

Roosevelt said, "The only thing we have to fear is fear itself." And the President's own confidence made the people more confident. He had a big grin and a booming laugh. He smoked cigarettes in a long holder and held it cocked at an angle in the corner of his mouth.

Roosevelt found it difficult to travel, so often Mrs. Roosevelt traveled for him. She went everywhere. She talked to people all over the country, then went home to tell the President what was needed. Eleanor Roosevelt became the best known and most widely loved of all the First Ladies.

In the election of 1936 Franklin Roosevelt carried every state in the Union but two. He kept on with his social reforms. Gradually times got better.

Roosevelt called his administration the "New Deal." He believed in

using the full power of the government to help what he called "the forgotten man." By this he meant the small businessman, the worker, the man in the street. And it was these people who came to love him most deeply. They felt that they knew him personally.

On the other hand there were many who honestly believed that Roosevelt's methods were destroying the American system of government. They hated him in the same personal way that other persons loved him. Many people would not even say his name. They called him "That madman in the White House."

By 1939 Roosevelt and the nation had a new problem to face. World War II began in Europe. Roosevelt, like most Americans, wanted the Allies to win. At the same time he hoped America could stay out of the war. As one country after another was defeated by the Germans, Roosevelt sent more and more supplies to the British.

In 1940 the Democrats nominated Roosevelt for a third term. No President had ever served three terms, not even Washington. Many persons believed no President should serve more than twice, although there was no law against it at that time. But Roosevelt did not want to quit while the nation was in danger. He loved power and he enjoyed being President. He accepted the nomination and won an easy victory.

On December 7, 1941, the Japanese bombed Pearl Harbor and America was plunged into the war. Now there were tremendous decisions to be made. Roosevelt met often with Winston Churchill, the British Prime Minister, and with other Allied leaders. They made the plans for war around the world.

In 1944 the war was still going on. Roosevelt was elected for the fourth time. But now the terrible strain and the long hours of work were telling on his health. His face had a gray look. Then his famous smile would flash and he would look strong again.

On April 12, 1945, Roosevelt was resting at his cottage in Warm Springs, Georgia. An artist was painting his picture. Suddenly he put a hand to his head and fell backward in his chair. A few hours later he was dead.

All over the world great men and common people alike mourned the President. In Europe, on ships at sea, in the jungles of the South Pacific, soldiers and sailors wept openly. As one sailor said, "It's tough when one of your buddies has to go, and President Roosevelt was our buddy." Many millions of people felt the same way.

Harry Truman

33rd President of the United States 1945-1953

Born: May 8, 1884, at Lamar, Missouri.

As a child, Harry Truman was often sick. By the time he was eight years old he had to wear glasses. He was so afraid he might break them that he rarely took part in the rough games of other boys. Instead, he spent much of his time reading. Before he was 14, he said later, he had read every book in the library at Independence, Missouri, where the family now lived.

Truman did not go to college. He worked for a railroad, a bank and on the family farm. He was 33 when World War I began. He promptly volunteered and went to France as a captain of artillery.

When the war was over he came home and married his childhood sweetheart. Then he and a friend started a men's clothing store in Kansas City. It failed. Truman could have declared bankruptcy and paid only part of what he owed. Instead, he paid off all his debts.

Because he was out of a job, Truman decided to go into politics. At this time the most powerful politician in Missouri was a man named Tom Pendergast. Much later Pendergast would be sent to prison for cheating on his income tax as well as fixing elections. But at this time it was almost impossible to be elected in Truman's home county without Pendergast's help. Harry Truman asked for Pendergast's help and got it. He was elected County Judge—a job that in most states would be called County Commissioner. He attracted state wide attention by making sure—to most people's surprise—that the roads in his county were honestly built.

In 1934 Truman was elected to the U.S. Senate, again with Pendergast's help. When the war began he became chairman of a committee to check on how money was spent on buying government supplies. He did an excellent job that saved the country more than a billion dollars.

When Roosevelt ran for his fourth term in 1944 there were several important men who wanted to be Vice President. President Roosevelt did not want to choose between them so he asked that Harry Truman be nominated instead. But after the election Roosevelt gave Truman very little to do. Roosevelt didn't even bother to tell him much about what was going on.

Then, suddenly, Roosevelt died and Truman was President.

All over the country people wondered what kind of President he would make. Back in Missouri he had been elected with the help of one of the nation's most crooked political groups. Now would he be loyal to the group or to his country?

For Truman himself there was never any doubt. He loved his country. He was fiercely proud of it. He was stunned by the size of the job facing him, but he was determined to do his best.

The war in Europe ended less than a month after Truman took office. He went to Europe to help draw up the peace. With this job he had help, but on the way home he was faced with one of the most terrible decisions any man has had to make. The United States had developed the atom bomb. Should it be used on Japan or not? The President had to decide.

Truman gave orders to drop the bomb. Two Japanese cities were destroyed before Japan surrendered. But it is almost certain that if the bomb had not been used, the United States would have had to invade Japan. Many more people, Americans as well as Japanese, would have been killed in the fighting.

Truman asked Congress for civil rights laws and to increase the social security. But Congress rarely passed the laws he asked for.

In 1948 Truman ran for election as President. The newspapers and the polls predicted he would be badly defeated. But Truman traveled back and forth across the country. He made more than 350 speeches. And to almost everyone's surprise, he won.

World War II was over, but the Cold War with Russia had begun. Once more Truman was faced by tremendous decisions. The Russians tried to force the Allies out of Berlin by blocking the roads and railroads across Russian-held territory. Truman ordered supplies flown in. For months the Berlin Airlift, as it was called, brought in everything from food to coal. Finally the Russians gave in and opened the roads.

Communists tried to overthrow the government of Greece. Truman declared that the United States would help free countries fighting to stay free of Communism. This was called the Truman Doctrine. It saved Greece and other countries. Under Truman's leadership the United States helped free European countries rebuild houses and factories that had been destroyed in the war.

After the war Korea had been divided in two parts. The northern half was under Communist control; the southern half was to be democratic. In June, 1950, Communists from the north invaded southern Korea. Immediately Truman ordered American troops to go to Korea. Then he asked for and got the help of the United Nations to save South Korea.

People who did not like Truman said he was not dignified enough to be President. There was some truth in the charge. He swore a lot. He liked to play poker, and he lost his temper too easily.

Sometimes his behavior was not worthy of a President of the United States. But history has shown that on the big decisions Harry Truman was nearly always right.

Dwight Eisenhower

34th President of the United States 1953-1961

Born: October 14, 1890, at Denison, Texas.

Young Dwight Eisenhower had his heart set on going to the Naval Academy at Annapolis. He wanted to be a sailor. But the examination

he took to enter Annapolis was the same required for the army school at West Point. So on his paper he had to mark one of three choices: Army, Navy, or Either.

Eisenhower marked the word "Either." When his appointment came through, it was to West Point.

At West Point Eisenhower played football until he hurt his knee. He was not big, but he was fast, lean and hard. He had a big grin and great personal charm. His team mates called him by his nickname, Ike. His class grades were average.

During World War I Eisenhower was a training officer in the United States. Later he served on the staff of General John Pershing and General Douglas MacArthur. When World War II began he was asked to draw up plans for war in the Pacific. These were so good that President Roosevelt promoted him over 366 other officers to head the U.S. Armies in Europe. Soon he was made Commander of all the Allied Forces in Europe.

This was a job that called for much more than just military skill. Eisenhower had to get along with generals from half a dozen countries. Also, he had to get along with the politicians who headed these countries. Only his skill, his tact, and great personal charm made the job possible.

After the war Eisenhower retired from the army and was appointed President of Columbia University. In 1948 both political parties wanted him to run for President. He refused. He said he did not believe a professional military man should be President.

The politicians kept after him. And in 1952 he agreed to run on the Republican ticket.

Eisenhower was not a good public speaker. He sometimes stumbled over his words. His sentences got tangled up. But he was obviously, totally honest. He had a big grin that made people feel they knew him personally. And everybody liked him. Even people who usually voted Democratic wore buttons that said I LIKE IKE. He won an easy victory to become the first Republican President in 20 years.

Eisenhower's great hope was that as President he could work for peace. He had seen enough war, he said. Now he would fight for peace.

At this time the war in Korea was still going on between United Nations forces and the Communists. Immediately after his election Eisenhower flew to Korea. It was largely through his efforts that peace was made a few months later.

Eisenhower tried hard to find some way to get along better with the

Russians. He wanted to end the danger of war. He said America would stop testing atomic weapons if the Russians would also. He set up a plan called Atoms For Peace to help smaller nations. Few of these ideas worked because the Russians would not agree.

At home Eisenhower did not make many changes in the policies begun by Presidents Roosevelt and Truman. He broadened the Social Security System and the Minimum Wage Law. He started a new system of national highways.

In 1955 Eisenhower had a heart attack. But he recovered quickly and next year was elected to a second term by a huge majority.

Eisenhower believed wholeheartedly in equal rights for all citizens. He completed the integration of the armed forces started by Roosevelt and Truman. He asked Congress for new civil rights laws. He did not, however, work as hard for these and other laws as Roosevelt and Truman. Because of this he was not regarded as a "strong" President. But when the opportunity came, he made his position clear. When the Governor of Arkansas refused to obey the law to integrate the high school in Little Rock, Eisenhower called out the army and forced the Governor to obey.

At the end of his second term Eisenhower was 70 years old, the oldest man ever to be President. He was happy to retire to a farm he had bought near Gettysburg, Pennsylvania. Because so much of his life had been spent in the army, it was the first home he and Mrs. Eisenhower had ever owned.

John Kennedy

35th President of the United States 1961-1963

Born: May 29, 1917, at Brookline, Massachusetts.
Died: November 22, 1963, at Dallas, Texas.

John Kennedy's father was a business man who made a huge fortune. He had nine children (John was the second oldest) and he gave each one of them a million dollars when they became 21. He also planned what his sons should do. Joe Kennedy Junior, the oldest boy, was to be the family politician. John—his family called him Jack—was to be a writer and teacher. He went to Harvard.

When World War II began, John Kennedy joined the Navy. He was the skipper of a PT Boat in the South Pacific. During a night battle a Japanese destroyer rammed into his small boat, cutting it in half. Two men were killed and Kennedy's back was badly hurt. Despite his own injury, Kennedy swam for hours towing another man even more badly hurt to a nearby island.

Joseph Kennedy, Jr., the brother who had planned to go into politics, was killed during the war. So the family decided that John would take his place. He ran for Congress—and the whole family pitched in to help. His brothers and brothers-in-law made speeches. His sisters and sisters-in-law gave teas. They invited thousands of people. They made thousands of telephone calls.

Kennedy was elected easily. He served three terms in the House of Representatives. Then he was elected to the Senate.

The war-time injury to Kennedy's back was still bothering him and he had to have an operation. While he was getting well he wrote a book called *Profiles in Courage* about United States Senators who had risked their careers to fight for things they believed in. The book won a prize as the best American history of that year.

From the first Kennedy had planned to run for President. In 1956 he tried for the Democratic Vice Presidential nomination but lost. Right away he started working toward the next election. As usual his whole family helped. Since they were all wealthy, money was no problem. They traveled back and forth across the country. They made speeches and talked with politicians. John Kennedy himself worked hardest of the lot. And when the Democratic Convention met, he was nominated for President on the first ballot.

Kennedy was 43 years old. Many people thought he was too young to be President. They thought he did not have enough experience. But the election of 1960 was the first time the candidates debated with one another on television. This was a big help to Kennedy. He was not only handsome but had great personal charm. He was also smart. He studied hard and had his facts ready. He spoke well and did not get flustered.

The election was one of the closest in history, but Kennedy won.

As President, Kennedy brought many teachers, writers and scientists into the government. Many of them worked for less money than they had made before. But they were willing to do this because they admired Kennedy. They believed in the things he wanted to do.

President Kennedy established the Peace Corps to help undeveloped countries. He worked hard for new civil rights laws. He wanted to

improve United States relations with Latin America. Congress, however, did not approve of most of Kennedy's plans.

Kennedy hoped the United States could have more friendly relations with Russia. At first, however, things got worse instead of better. Cuba, under Fidel Castro, had already turned Communist. And in October, 1962, Kennedy learned that the Russians were sending missiles to Cuba. With atomic warheads they could destroy cities all across the United States.

President Kennedy acted promptly. He ordered the navy to blockade Cuba so no more Russian ships could enter. He sent planes and soldiers to Florida to be ready to invade Cuba if necessary. Over the television he told the American people what had happened. He explained the grave danger of war. He was asking the Russian leader, he said, "to halt and eliminate this . . . threat to world peace."

For one week the United States and Russia seemed on the edge of war. Then the Russians backed down. They took their missiles out of Cuba. After that relations with Russian did become a little better.

On November 22, 1963, Kennedy was to make a speech in Dallas, Texas. As he rode through the street, sitting beside his wife, a shot rang out. The President fell forward, dead.

The entire nation was stunned at the President's death. Because he was so young and vital the people mourned him as they had mourned no President since Lincoln.

Lyndon Johnson

36th President of the United States 1963-

Born: August 27, 1908, near Stonewall, Texas.

It was natural enough for Lyndon Johnson to become a politician. Both his father and grandfather had been members of the Texas Legislature. The day Lyndon was born his grandfather mounted his horse and went galloping around the county. "A United States Senator has just been born!" he shouted at his friends.

Lyndon's father and mother were both school teachers. They taught Lyndon to read by the time he was four. In school he made good

grades. But when he finished high school he felt he had had enough school. He was six feet three inches tall, skinny, and restless. He was always moving, trying to do two or three things at one time. But he did not yet know just what he really wanted to do. So he traveled around the country, working at odd jobs.

Finally he went back home. "I'm sick of working with my hands," he told his parents. "I don't know if I can work with my brain, but I'm ready to try."

He went to college. He made good grades. And he became interested in campus politics. He organized a political party that won all the campus elections.

After college Johnson taught school. But he could not leave politics. He worked for a man named Robert Kleberg who was running for Congress. Kleberg was elected and took Johnson to Washington as his secretary.

Working for Kleberg, Johnson had to travel back and forth to Texas. On one of these trips he met Claudia Taylor. Everybody called her Lady Bird, a nickname given to her when she was two years old. Within a few months Lyndon Johnson and Lady Bird were married.

When Johnson was 29 years old he ran for Congress on his own and was elected. A few years later when the Japanese bombed Pearl Harbor, Johnson quickly asked for active duty in the navy. He was the first member of Congress to go into uniform.

After the war Johnson was elected to the U. S. Senate. He proved to be of the best Senators in history. He had a great gift for getting people with different ideas to work together.

In 1960 Johnson was elected Vice President along with President Kennedy. When Kennedy was killed November 22, 1963, Johnson became President. To the American people he promised to carry on with Kennedy's plans. He said, "I will do my best. That is all I can do. I ask for your help—and God's."

During his first year as President, Johnson pushed many important bills through Congress. Then in 1964 he was elected President by a huge majority.

Under Johnson's leadership Congress passed new civil rights laws. One of these guaranteed Negroes the right to vote. This had been denied them in some Southern states. "To deny a man his hopes because of color or race, his religion or place of birth," President Johnson said, "is not only to do injustice, it is to deny America and dishonor the dead who gave their lives for freedom."

Johnson began what he called a "War On Poverty" to improve city slums and other poor sections of the country. He got Congress to pass a Medicare law. This helped old people pay their medical bills. He got laws to slow down the pollution of American rivers and air, and laws to make highways more beautiful.

Not everyone approved of the laws Johnson passed. Some people said the civil rights laws gave Negroes too many rights. Some people said they did not give enough. Race riots started in a number of cities, and each side blamed the other.

In foreign affairs the big problem that faced President Johnson was in South Viet Nam. Here, for many years, Communists from North Viet Nam had been fighting to take over the country. President Eisenhower had sent American soldiers to advise the soldiers of South Viet Nam. President Kennedy had sent still more. But South Viet Nam was still losing the war. So President Johnson sent more and more United States soldiers. These soldiers took more and more part in the fighting.

Many Americans thought the United States had no business in Viet Nam. They wanted President Johnson to bring the soldiers home. Other Americans said the fight in Viet Nam was part of a world-wide fight against Communism. They wanted President Johnson to send a huge army to South Viet Nam. They wanted to bomb North Viet Nam off the map and end the war.

President Johnson's stand was in the middle. He did not want to destroy North Viet Nam. Time and again he tried to make peace, but only if the Communists would leave South Viet Nam alone. And the Communists would not agree.

Most Americans agreed with the President. But the fighting went on and on, and nobody knew how it would end.